FINANCIAL FREEDOM WITH REAL ESTATE

Start Making Money Today Because Everyone Else Is

3 SIMPLE WAYS THAT EVEN YOUR KIDS CAN DO IT: SECRETS GUARANTEED TO WORK RIGHT AWAY

Written by

MICHAEL STEVEN

CONTENTS

FINANCIAL FREEDOM CHECKLIST

(A Simple list that should be followed to the "T")

This checklist includes:

❏ 9 important steps that you should follow to achieve success and head toward *Financial Freedom With Real Estate*

❏ Plus receive future updates

Forget about yesterday and start thinking about tomorrow!

"The past and the future are separated by a second,
so make that second count!"
—Carmine Pirone

To receive your Financial Freedom With Real Estate checklist, email me at:

michael@TheBestSellerBooks.com

INTRODUCTION

"Real estate cannot be lost or stolen, nor can it be carried away. Purchased with common sense, paid for in full, and managed with reasonable care, it is about the safest investment in the world."
—*Franklin D Roosevelt*

Ever thought about getting out of the rat race and achieving financial independence?

Today, we live in a world where it is no longer possible to rely solely on your job to sustain yourself and your family. The cost of living has been rising steadily while wages have remained stagnant. To make matters worse, employees have become highly expendable, especially in times of crisis, as shown by the COVID-19 pandemic that has taken the world by storm.

In a bid to survive, businesses and companies across the country have had no other option but to lay off employees. According to the U.S. Department of Labor, over 30 million Americans (about 18% of the U.S. labor force) filed for unemployment benefits in the period between March and

May 2020. The United States has not experienced such high levels of unemployment since the 1930s. These numbers show that, if you rely solely on employment, you can find yourself out in the cold easily in case of a crisis.

To make matters worse, with these stagnated wages and the rising cost of living, most jobs today do not even allow people to save enough money for retirement. Most working-age Americans have savings totaling less than $10,000. This amount is way too little, considering how estimates show that, to retire comfortably, millennials will need savings of about $2.5 million. This disparity between what one needs to retire comfortably and what most Americans have saved up means that the majority of the population will likely be unable to retire. Actually, according to the Employee Benefit Research Institute, 80% of Americans plan to continue working past their retirement age. The question is, how feasible is this option? By the time they are in their 70s and 80s, a lot of people usually have to deal with a myriad of health problems, which means that working at that age is not a feasible solution.

In addition to the risk of being laid off at any minute and not earning quite enough money to save for retirement, relying solely on a job to support yourself keeps you from pursuing your dreams. After all, if you spend all your time in the office, when will you ever get the time to chase after your dreams? Smart people understand that to pursue one's dreams, they first need to free themselves from their job. A good example of such a person is a renowned actor and former California governor, Arnold Schwarzenegger.

For a long time, Schwarzenegger had a passion for acting and knew he would get into it at one point. However, Schwarzenegger had observed something important in the movie industry: actors who relied solely on movies for a living did not have much control over their lives. Since this was the source of their livelihood, such actors were forced to take anything that came their way, including crappy roles in crappy movies, since this was the only way for them to survive. This is not the kind of life Schwarzenegger wanted for himself.

Therefore, Schwarzenegger focused first on creating another source of livelihood. He invested in real estate, and, within a short time, his real estate investments made him a millionaire. Confident that he now had a source of income that didn't require his full-time focus, Schwarzenegger could then focus on pursuing his dreams of becoming a movie star. Since he wasn't desperate for roles, he was able to achieve success quickly in the movie industry. Over the course of his acting career, Schwarzenegger won a Golden Globe Award and got nominated for several other awards, with his movies grossing a total of over $1.7 billion.

If you want to have financial security, even in times of crisis, enough money to retire comfortably, and enough freedom to pursue your dreams, you have to stop relying solely on your day job; instead, start thinking of achieving financial freedom. The best way to do this is to start investing your money. Although there are several available options you can look into when it comes to investing, one of the best ways to invest your money is to get into real estate.

Real estate has consistently been one of the best performing investments over the last couple of decades, performing even better than the stock market. It is not surprising that the majority of millionaires in the United States have their investments in the real estate sector because real estate has delivered consistently good returns to investors over the last few centuries. According to The College Investor, real estate investments have played a significant role in creating wealth for over 90% of millionaires.

Even millennials have realized that investing in real estate is one of the best ways of building wealth. According to a 2019 report by Coldwell Banker, the typical millennial millionaire believes that owning real estate is key to creating wealth, with the average millennial millionaire having invested in three properties.

Though many people know that investing in real estate is a great way to build wealth, a lot of them are still reluctant about putting their money into real estate. This happens for a couple of reasons—first, many see real estate as a complex industry that requires lots of insider knowledge to get into. In addition, most assume that to get into real estate, you need to start with millions. However, the truth is that getting into real estate is a lot easier than you think.

If you have considered getting out of a dead-end job and achieving financial freedom through real estate investing but did not know where to start, this book is for you. You may probably even have a few other investments in stocks, bonds, and other instruments, and you want to diversify your investments into real estate. However, you may not have enough knowledge to allow yourself to put your money confidently into the real estate sector. You may have asked yourself one of the following questions:

- Is there a way to become financially free in my current situation?
- Can I afford to buy real estate for investment?
- How do I make money from real estate?
- How do I start investing in real estate?
- What should I know before I start?

If this sounds like you, you have come to the right place. Whether you have had some experience buying a home but want to expand into investing to make enough money to live comfortably, or are a novice who has never purchased property before, this book will teach you everything you need to know about real estate investing. It offers useful tools and strategies that anyone can use for real estate investing, even if you don't have millions of dollars in savings, and breaks down complex real estate jargon into simple concepts that can be understood, even by kids. The book details all the important steps to take when making your first real estate investment and breaks down the thought process that goes into choosing a property.

Some of the things you will learn in this book include:

- The importance of financial independence in helping you pursue and achieve your dreams and goals.
- How to get out of the mindset that financial freedom is unachievable or that you have to work until you are in your 60s or 70s to be able to retire.
- The basics of real estate and real estate investing, and how it can help you build wealth.
- A step-by-step guide to getting started with real estate investing, including how to crunch the numbers and ensure that your investment will actually pay off, how to finance and pay for your real estate investments, how to manage them, and, most importantly, how to profit from them.
- How to increase your real estate portfolio until you reach financial independence.
- And so much more!

At this point, you may be wondering who I am and if I am qualified enough to teach you about how to achieve financial freedom with real estate. After all, you don't want to be taking advice from a quack. My name is Michael Steven, and I am a real estate investor. Before getting into real estate, I used to sell my time for money. In other words, I worked for others and, while they were making money with my time, I was running out of it. When people say "time is money," they are lying because time is priceless. Despite being in a high-paying job, the desire to upgrade my lifestyle constantly and live a life of luxury resulted in a situation where I was constantly struggling to make ends meet. Before I knew it, I had accumulated a significant amount of debt. I decided to use my strengths and knowledge and started to work for a bank to help people with their finances. I became a mortgage specialist and a very successful one. I was making more money than I could have imagined, but there was one thing still missing—that's right, time for *myself*. As a matter of fact, I had less time at that point than I ever had. That's when I decided that I had to find another way to make time for myself, and the only answer was in real estate.

It was at this point that I realized that, if I didn't make changes to my life, I would never be happy and eventually run out of time and would have lost time with my family as well. I approached a friend who was already investing in real estate, and through his help, I learned how I could also start investing, despite the lack of time. Slowly, I started making changes to my life and made an investment in a small duplex.

From there, I have gradually expanded my portfolio; today, I own multiple properties that bring me more money than I would have imagined I would ever make. I managed to make more time and enjoy life with my wife and three kids.

Knowing how challenging it is to be in the situation I was once in, I decided to write this book as a way to give back to society and share the knowledge that helped me turn my life around. My hope is to help other people who are stuck in a rut take control over their lives and achieve financial freedom.

Unlike most other books you may have come across, the strategies and knowledge shared in this book are not just theoretical concepts. They are the actual strategies that took me from mountains of debt and a paycheck-to-paycheck lifestyle to financial freedom, and a life where I can do whatever I want without having to worry about how I will be taking care of next month's bills. Since these strategies worked for me, you can be sure that they will work for you too, provided you put in the work and apply everything you learn from this book.

Are you excited about embarking on your journey to financial freedom? Let's get started.

CHAPTER ONE: FINANCIAL FREEDOM IS CLOSER THAN YOU THINK

D o you spend your time fantasizing about living the life of your dreams, but then feel powerless to do anything about it because you are scared of leaving your soul-sucking job when you don't have another reliable source of income? Do you wish you had the time and freedom to travel around the world, spend time with your family, or focus on your passions and personal projects? Do you wish you had enough money to retire whenever you wanted, instead of waiting until you turn 60, then retiring to a miserable life living off your pension?

The truth is that all these things are possible. It *is* possible to live your life on your own terms, follow your dreams, and even retire at whatever age you wanted, even at 30. The key to living such a life lies in achieving financial independence.

So, what exactly does financial independence mean?

Financial independence refers to a situation in which you are not dependent on income sources that require you to exchange your time for money. Instead, the income you need for your survival comes from passive sources. For instance, someone whose sole income comes from a job is not financially independent. If they were to stop working for a month, they would be unable to meet their needs the following month because they no longer have an income. Someone who is financially independent, on the other hand, doesn't need to trade their time for money. This means that such a person can do whatever they wanted and would still have money in their bank at the end of the month. Such a person has already made investments in assets that automatically generate enough money for them to cover their living expenses.

Attaining financial freedom has several benefits. Since you are not dependent on a job to cover your living expenses, financial freedom gives you control over your time. You can spend your time however you want—whether that means traveling the world, golfing all day, spending time with your family, or even sleeping. In addition, financial freedom allows you to pursue your passions. Very often, people are unable to pursue their passions because they don't pay well enough.

For instance, your passion might be writing novels, but then it would take you too long to get to a point where you can live off your books comfortably. To make matters worse, there is no guarantee you will actually make enough money from your novels. In such a situation, you would be forced to take a job you didn't love, just to make the money you need to survive. Unfortunately, this job might end up taking so much of your time that you won't have any time to write novels. On the other hand, if you were financially independent, you would have the freedom to focus on your passion for writing novels, even if the novels weren't making enough money for you to live on.

For most people, the concept of financial independence and never having to worry about money is a dream they would want to achieve, and many of them actually strive to get there.

Imagine having this kind of life: you wake up in the morning, not in a rush to get ready for work and beat the morning traffic, but to a luxurious, relaxed breakfast with your family. You read the papers for an hour, then spend the next hour on the phone talking with your managers and financial advisors, getting updates on how your investments are doing. Once you confirm that everything is going well with your investments, you can join some friends for a game of golf. In the afternoon, you would spend time working on one of your hobbies—whether that is painting, playing an instrument, writing, you name it. Every summer, you get to take your family on vacation to a tropical island and get to spend your days sipping on mojitos and piña coladas while you watch your kids frolicking on the white, sandy beaches. All this without having to worry about money or limited leave days. Wouldn't you want such a life?

The truth is that most people would want that life, though many do struggle to build such a life. However, for a lot of them, this kind of life doesn't go beyond just being a dream. This is because you can't just get to wake up one morning and start living such a life. Such a life, a life of financial freedom, is the result of careful planning and deliberate action. Those who live such lifestyles got there through lots of hard work and making smart moves.

The good thing, however, is that, if you know what to do, and if you actually commit to doing it, you can attain financial independence. Below are some of the things you need to do if you want to be financially independent.

Start Spending Less Than You Earn

When I used to work as a consultant for a top management firm, I was earning quite a high salary, yet I was in debt and living paycheck to paycheck. The problem was not how much I was earning; it was how I used to spend my money. Eager to live a flashy lifestyle, I used to purchase things I couldn't afford, which is why I found myself in debt.

If you want to attain financial independence, the first thing you need to do is to start living within your means, which means spending less than you earn. Without doing this, it is impossible to become financially independent, regardless of how much money you make. Ideally, you should aim for a situation in which you get to save at least 30% of your monthly income. Therefore, if you have been spending beyond your income, the first thing you need to do is to find ways to start spending less, which brings us to my second point.

Cut Down Your Expenses

If you have been spending more than you earn, the best way to start spending less is to cut down your expenses. You also have the option of increasing your income, though this is a lot harder than cutting expenses. Even if you have been spending less than you earn, cutting down on your expenses will allow you to save more money.

To cut down your expenses, you need to know where your money goes. Start by tracking everything you spend your money on every month. Once you have a good idea of where your money is going, go through the list and identify some expenses that are unnecessary, or those you can cut back on. For instance, if you pay money for the gym, but you rarely ever set foot in the gym, you need to cut down on that expense. If you are making car repayments, you could sell the car and find a cheaper one with lower repayments. You may even purchase a cheap used car that you can afford without taking on debt. If you live in an expensive apartment, consider moving to a smaller, less costly apartment. Basically, if you have any unnecessary expenses, get rid of them, and find ways to reduce the cost of your necessary expenses.

Pay Off Debt

If you want to become financially independent, you also need to pay off any debt you owe. There are several reasons why you should focus on repaying your debt. First, having lots of debt means that you will have equally high payments to make every month. Once you reduce your debt, your loan payments will also go down, leaving you with more money to save. For instance, if you were making debt payments worth $600 each month, lowering your debt might lower your monthly loan payments to $300. This results in an extra $300 in your account every month, or about $3,600 every year. If you clear all of your debt, you will have an extra $600 each month, or about $7200 every year.

The second reason why you need to pay off your debt is that debt costs you money. The longer you take before clearing your debt, the more money you will end up paying in interest charges. This is money you could have saved by clearing your debt.

Finally, paying off your debt will lead to an improvement in various indicators of your financial health, such as your credit score. This will, in turn, make it easier for you to get access financing in the future. For instance, if you decide to invest in real estate, but don't have enough money saved up to pay for a property, a good credit score will make it easier for you to get financing.

Find Ways to Increase Your Income

Now that you have cut down your expenses and paid off your debt, start thinking of ways through which you can increase your income. You can do this by asking for a pay raise at your current job, starting a side hustle, finding a new job that pays better, renting off a room in your house on Airbnb, selling off stuff in your home that you no longer need, and so on. One thing to note here is that, while you are increasing your income, you need to watch out to ensure you don't increase your expenses as well. The reason you are increasing your income is to allow yourself to save even more money every month.

Make the Right Investments

All the previous steps have been focused on ensuring that you have more money to save each month. However, you are not saving this money just for the sake of it. The money you are saving will act as the foundation that will allow you to attain financial freedom, which will only happen if you invest the money you have saved up. Investing is what allows your money to multiply. There are several ways through which you can invest your money, such as purchasing stocks, bonds, trading in commodities, peer-to-peer lending, putting your money into mutual funds, high yield savings accounts, and so on. However, one of the best ways of investing your money is putting it into real estate. This is the quickest way of growing your money and attaining financial independence.

Like I mentioned in the introduction to this book, most millionaires have investments in the real estate sector, and a lot of them attribute their wealth to returns from their real estate investments. Some of the richest people in the world who made their wealth through investing in real estate include Chinese billionaire Wang Jianlin, who has an empire valued at over $28.7 billion; Lee Shau Kee, whose empire is in excess of $21.5 billion; German billionaire Michael Otto, who is worth $15.4 billion; and American billionaires Donald Bren, Stephen Ross, and David Lichtenstein, who have a net worth of $15.1 billion, $12 billion, and $1.45 billion respectively.

There are several other famous people who have portions of their wealth invested in real estate, including Diddy, Ellen DeGeneres, Nas, Roberto De Niro, Jay Z, 50 Cent, Leonardo DiCaprio, Arnold Schwarzenegger, Brad Pitt, and so many more.

Some of the reasons why all these people choose to invest in real estate include:

- **Real estate provides predictable cash flow:** One of the best things about investing is that it generates predictable and sustainable cash flow. Cash flow refers to the net income from your property that you are left with after taking out operating expenses and mortgage payments. Actually, this is the main reason why most people invest in real estate. Unlike many other investment options, where you have to liquidate the investment to realize its gains, a real estate investment puts money into your pocket every month—consistently and predictably.

The best part about this is that all this money is generated passively. It doesn't require you to do much. You can find someone to manage your properties for you, make sure rent is paid on time, and perform routine maintenance tasks while you sit back and enjoy your money. Over time, you can expand your portfolio of properties to the point where you generate more money each month than you need for taking care of your expenses. When you get there, you will have achieved true financial independence.

- **Potential for capital appreciation:** In addition to

generating regular cash flow, real estate also tends to grow in value over time, thus giving you even more returns on your investment. For instance, let's say you purchase a property for $100,000 and hold it for a period of ten years. Over those ten years, the value of the property keeps rising. At the end of ten years, you sell it for $150,000. In this case, you would have made a profit of $50,000 through capital appreciation, in addition to all the cash flow the property has generated. Aside from capital appreciation, rental prices also tend to grow over time, which means even higher cash flow without any additional investment.

• **Tax advantages:** Investing in real estate can also give you access to tax benefits that are not available with other investment options. Real estate expenses such as property taxes, mortgage interest, property management fees are treated as business expenses, and are, therefore, tax-deductible. This means that the taxable income from your real estate investments will be lower. In addition, real estate investments are depreciable, which means your property taxes will go down over time. Depreciation allows property owners to account for the effect of wear and tear when valuing their property over time.

• **Lower risk in economic downturns:** During periods of economic downturns, the performance of most investments takes a hit. For instance, following the outbreak of COVID-19, global shares took a major hit. In the period between January and March 2020, the Dow Jones Industrial Average and the FTSE experienced the largest quarterly drops since 1987. So, if you had your money invested in the stock market or other financial instruments, you would probably have lost your money.

If you had your money invested in property, on the other hand, you probably wouldn't have felt the pinch. Whether there is a global crisis or the economy is performing well or not, people will still need somewhere to live. Therefore, if you own a portfolio of rental properties, they will continue generating cash flow, even if the economy is in recession.

- **Better potential for diversification:** Every financial advisor will tell you about the importance of diversification when it comes to investing your money. Diversification prevents your entire portfolio from getting wiped out in the event of a downturn in the market. It is a way of spreading out your risk. Real estate provides a great option for diversifying your investments because its correlation with most other asset classes is usually low, and sometimes negative. For instance, although the stock market has taken a hit as a result of the COVID-19 pandemic, real estate has not been greatly affected. Therefore, by investing some of your money in real estate, you are effectively lowering the volatility of your portfolio.

- **Real estate can be leveraged to build wealth:** Another major advantage of investing in real estate is that you can use it as leverage to build wealth. Leverage refers to the use of borrowed capital to boost the potential return of your investment. For instance, you can purchase a property by just putting down a 20% down payment. This is an example of leverage. Alternatively, if you already own one property, you can use it as collateral to secure financing to purchase another property. Most other investment options do not allow you to do this.

- **Real estate is a tangible asset that will always have value:** One of the best things about real estate is that it is a tangible asset, which means that it will always have value. If you invest in stocks, for instance, the investment might grow and make you wealthy, but you will only be wealthy on paper. An economic crisis can wipe out your entire investment within no time. With real estate, on the other hand, unless your property gets destroyed, it will always have value. You don't have to worry about waking up one day to find that your investments that were worth millions are now worthless.

Compute Living Budget and Expenses

Finally, to become financially independent, you will need to compute how much money you need to live comfortably. This amount will differ from person to person, depending on lifestyle, preferences, living arrangements, family size, and so on. Assuming you have already made an investment in a rental property, you will want to get in a position where your rental income can cater to all your living expenses. From there, as you expand your portfolio, your investments will generate more money than you need to survive, which will act as your launchpad on your journey to financial freedom.

By following these six steps, it is possible for anyone to build wealth and attain financial independence, regardless of financial situation. You just need to make a commitment to yourself to follow through with the six steps. In the next chapter, we will look at the basics of real estate investing, so you can be more aware of what you are getting into.

CHAPTER TWO: KNOW WHAT YOU ARE GETTING INTO: WHAT EXACTLY IS REAL ESTATE INVESTING?

In the previous chapter, we established that investing your money is a critical aspect of building wealth and attaining financial independence; and that one of the best things you can invest in is real estate. In this chapter, I will be taking you through the basics of real estate investing. The information you will learn in this chapter will lay the foundation for what you will learn through the rest of the book and help you navigate the ins and outs of real estate investing.

How People Make Money in Real Estate

The main reason you are investing in real estate is you want to multiply your money. The question is—how exactly do people make money investing in real estate?

Generally, people make money in real estate in two ways, which we will discuss in the next few sections.

Real Estate Appreciation

In the previous chapter, we saw that the value of real estate will continue growing over time. In other words, if you purchase some property and hold it for a substantial period —say about 5 years or more—you can then sell the property at a higher price than you bought it. This is what is known as appreciation.

There are several reasons that contribute to the appreciation of real estate. The first one is due to supply and demand. As the population continues growing, and as cities and towns grow, demand for land increases. However, land is a finite resource. This increasing demand for land against limited supply means that people will become more willing to pay more for land later than they are willing to pay today, leading to appreciation. Similarly, as cities grow, there is increased demand for residential and commercial properties, which leads to an increase both in the price and rent of these properties.

Another factor that leads to an appreciation of real estate is development and improvement. For instance, if you purchase an undeveloped piece of land and construct a building on it, the value of that land will go up automatically. Similarly, if you purchase a building and make improvements to it—such as increasing its square footage, repairing the roof, and adding various amenities—the value of the building will go up.

Improvement of the area surrounding the property can also trigger appreciation. For instance, let's say you purchase a piece of land in a remote area that is not served by public utilities. Over time, the local government installs public utilities in the area, such as power, natural gas, street lighting, piped water, and so on. While these improvements have not been made specifically on your piece of land, they can still result in an increase in value for your property. Similarly, other forms of growth in the area around your property—development of shopping centers, the addition of transit routes, development of more residential and commercial properties, development of schools and playgrounds, and so on—can also spur the appreciation of a piece of real estate.

Finally, appreciation can also be caused by the discovery of something valuable on a piece of land. For instance, if you purchase a piece of land and discover a valuable mineral on the plot, this will automatically drive up its value. Such appreciation can be driven by a variety of natural resources.

Data from the U.S. Department of Housing and Urban Development and the U.S. Census Bureau aggregated by the Federal Reserve Bank of St. Louis shows that the average sale prices of properties sold in the country have been on an upward trend from the 1970s. Though there are some brief periods where the average sales prices went down (during economic recessions), there is a high likelihood that this upward trend will continue.

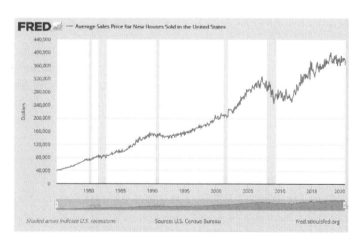

Image credit: Federal Reserve Bank of St. Louis

Aside from the potential profit from the appreciation of a property, the capital appreciation of real estate is also a great way of hedging your money against inflation. Inflation refers to the decrease in the purchasing power of money over time. To understand how the capital appreciation of real estate hedges against inflation, let's assume that you save $100,000 in a savings account for a period of 10 years. At the end of those 10 years, you will still have $100,000 in your account; however, you won't be able to buy as much with that $100,000 in 10 years as you would have been able to buy today since the price of items will have gone up. If the inflation rate for that period is 10%, the $100,000 will have lost 10% of its purchasing power, which means that, in 10 years, $100,000 can only buy items that would be worth $90,000 today.

Now, imagine someone else who also had $100,000 decided to purchase a property with that money rather than putting it in a savings account. That person then decides to sell off the property after 10 years. Assuming the appreciation rate over that period was 10%, this person will sell the property at $110,000. Assuming a similar rate of inflation, items that used to cost $100,000 will now cost $110,000. However, this person can still afford these items, unlike the one who kept their money in a savings account. Therefore, the person who invested in real estate will have hedged his money against inflation. Typically, the rate of appreciation for real estate is usually higher than the rate of inflation, which allows people with real estate investments to hedge their money against inflation and, at the same time, make a profit on capital appreciation.

It's good to note, however, that while the value of a property will constantly appreciate over the duration that you hold the property, the only way to realize profits from this appreciation is by selling said property. In addition, appreciation is quite unpredictable compared to the second way of making money through real estate, which is cash flow.

Cash Flow Income

Cash flow income refers to the money generated by a piece of property periodically and consistently, and less on the expenses of operating that property. Real estate generates cash flow income in one of two ways:

• **Rental income:** This refers to income generated from leasing out your property to tenants for a fixed sum of money every month. This is the most common way of generating cash flow income from a property. Rental income can be generated by both residential and commercial properties, along with storage units. For commercial properties, a property can also generate rental income in the form of option income. Option income refers to money paid by tenants on a commercial property for contractual options, such as relisting or first right of refusal options.

• **Raw land income:** If you own an undeveloped piece of land and hold all the rights to that parcel, you can get into a contract with a third party and have them pay you regular payments for putting up any structures on the land or royalties from any discoveries made on that piece of land. For instance, you can get into a contract with a telecommunications company, allowing them to put up a cell tower on your land in exchange for regular payments, or you could get into a contract with a mining company and have them pay you royalties for mining gravel from your land. Alternatively, you can lease out your land to be used for agricultural production.

The best thing about cash flow income—both rental income and raw land income—is that it provides you with a passive source of income. It guarantees you a regular income without requiring you to do much. For instance, if you lease out your land to a telecommunications company for erecting a cell tower, you don't have to do much, yet you will continue receiving the regular payments for the duration of your contract.

It is also good to note that, regardless of the route you choose for making money from your real estate investments, the amount you can make from your investments will be determined by several external factors, which you will need to take into consideration before investing in a property.

Factors that Affect the Real Estate Market

Some factors that affect the real estate market and the amount of money you can make by investing in real estate include:

- **Demographics:** Demographics refers to details pertaining to the composition of the population within an area, such as the average age of the population, their income levels, racial background, population growth, migration patterns, and so on. These details affect the performance of the real estate market in several ways. For instance, a majorly young population will have a different preference for housing compared to a majorly old and retired population. Similarly, the preferences of a population with a low average income will be different from those of a population with a high average income. In addition, trends like population growth and migration also affect the demand for housing.

• **Interest rates:** If you are taking a mortgage to finance your purchase of a property, the prevailing interest rates will affect the amount of money you can make from your investment. Higher interest rates will lead to higher monthly payments, which translates to lower cash flow from your property. Even for those purchasing property with the intention of flipping the property for a profit, interest rates can also affect your ability to make money. For instance, an increase in interest rates will make it more difficult for people to obtain mortgages, which will then lead to decreased demand for real estate and thus lower prices.

• **The economy:** The performance of the economy also has an effect on the performance of the real estate market. Poor performance in the economy means less money in people's pockets, leading to decreased demand for housing.

• **Government policies:** When investing in real estate, it is good to watch out for government policies, since they have an effect on the demand and prices of real estate. By offering subsidies and tax credits, for instance, the government can increase demand for real estate. A good example of this is what the U.S. government did back in 2009: in a bid to boost demand for real estate following the 2008 economic recession, the government introduced a tax credit to first time home buyers. This tax credit resulted in over 900,000 people purchasing homes. Being aware of such government policies can help you identify the best time to invest in real estate.

Risks Associated with Investing in Real Estate

In addition to watching out for the above factors that can

influence your ability to make money from real estate, it is also good to note that, as with any other investment, there are some inherent risks to investing in real estate. It is important to be aware of these risks to prepare for and minimize them.

Some of the risks associated with investing in real estate include:

• **Purchasing a bad property:** One of the worst mistakes you can make when investing in real estate is to purchase a property that has some hidden problems you were unaware of, such as a roof that needs repair, mold issues, structural issues, or defective appliances. Such problems will require you to sink more money than you had anticipated into the property, which will then affect the profitability of your investment. To avoid this, the best thing to do is hire professional home inspectors and make sure every element of the property has been examined thoroughly before going ahead with your purchase.

• **Negative cash flow:** If you don't get the numbers right when evaluating a property you want to invest in, you can easily end up purchasing a property that requires more money to operate and maintain than it can generate from rental income. In such a situation, you will actually be losing money. To prevent this, you should be careful when crunching the numbers before you make the purchase. You need to make sure that the potential rental income from the property will be enough to cover expenses, like mortgage payments, management fees, maintenance costs, and taxes, and leave a significant amount of profit. Techniques such as the 1% rule will help you determine the potential profitability of a property before you put down your money. We'll go over these techniques in greater detail in the next chapter.

• **Bad tenants:** Investing in real estate also comes with the risk of bad tenants. These are tenants who do not pay their rent on time, cause damages and destruction to your property, are a nuisance to their neighbors, and so on. To avoid such tenants, you need to screen potential tenants thoroughly before allowing them into your property. I will cover the process of screening your tenants in Chapter 5.

• **Vacancy risk:** Once you have invested in a property, there is no guarantee your property will be fully occupied at all times. Of course, the vacancy will affect your profitability, and the higher the vacancy rates, the lower your profits. High vacancy rates can even result in negative cash flow. You can reduce vacancy risk by investing in properties that are located in a good location with lots of demand for housing and ensuring your property is always in good condition.

• **A decrease in property value:** While I mentioned that the value of a property would generally appreciate, there are some situations when properties might decrease in value. For instance, during the 2008 economic crisis, the value of properties took a major tumble. If you had purchased a property with the intention of flipping it quickly, you would have been at risk of selling it at a loss or being forced to hold the property for longer than you expected. However, the risk of a decrease in value is not very high, especially if your intention is to hold the property over the long term and generate cash flow from rental income.

• **Wrong location:** Choosing the right location is one of the most important considerations you should keep in mind before investing in a property. The biggest problem with choosing the wrong location is the low demand for housing, which means having to deal with high vacancy rates, lower rent prices, and so on, all of which can affect the profitability of your property. Therefore, it is important to research an area carefully before purchasing a property in that area. I will look at the process of researching areas more extensively in the next chapter.

While it may not be possible to eliminate these risks completely, knowing about and recognizing them will help you minimize them, and, with proper and thorough research, the benefits of investing in real estate will far outweigh the risks.

The Different Types of Real Estate You Can Invest In

When most people think of real estate investing, they typically think about one type of real estate: residential real estate. However, there are many other types you can invest in too. Knowing the different types can help you figure out the best type of real estate for you to invest in. The following are the four major types of real estate:

• **Residential Real Estate:** This is the most common and most popular real estate asset: class. Residential real estate refers to buildings that are constructed with the objective of housing people, either individually or as families. Some common types of residential real estate include single-family homes, condos, duplexes, triplexes, quadplexes, and townhouses.

- **Commercial Real Estate:** This refers to land and buildings that are set aside for business purposes. Some examples of commercial real estate include shopping malls, office buildings, hotels, education, and medical buildings. It's good to note that, while apartments are used for residential purposes, they can also be considered as commercial real estate because they are developed to generate income for the owner.

- **Industrial Real Estate:** This refers to land and buildings that are used for purposes such as research, manufacturing, and storage of goods. Examples of industrial real estate include factories, research and development centers, and warehouses.

- **Land**: This refers to undeveloped land. The land can either be vacant, or it can be under agricultural use.

Different Ways of Investing in Real Estate

When it comes to investing in real estate, you have several options available to you. The best option for you will depend on what you want to achieve from your investment, finances, the effort you are willing to expend on your investment, and so on. Below are some common ways through which you can invest in real estate.

Purchasing Real Estate Investment Trusts

This is probably the easiest way of getting into real estate investing. Real estate investment trusts, also known as REITs, are basically like mutual funds that own and operate commercial real estate. By purchasing a REIT, you become a shareholder of the company, owning and operating the real estate. You are, therefore, also entitled to your share of profits from the real estate. This share of profits is paid in the form of dividends.

The beauty of REITs is that they make it possible for you to invest in real estate without having to own the actual property. As a new investor, if you decide to invest in REITs, you should go for publicly traded REITs over non-traded REITs. Non-traded REITs are harder to buy, sell, and value.

Purchasing Rental Properties

The second and more traditional way of investing in real estate is to purchase a residential property with the aim of earning rental income. With this option, you have several options. The first one is to purchase a single-family home and put it up for rent. Alternatively, you can purchase a multi-family property and live in one unit, while putting the other units up for rent. This allows you to cover your housing expenses and the mortgage on the house while still making an income from the property. You can also buy a multi-family property and put up all the units for rent.

Another option is to purchase a residential property and let it out over the short term through services like Airbnb. Prior to the COVID-19 pandemic, which has made it impossible for people to travel, there was a huge demand for vacation rentals. Although this market has declined, for now, it is likely to rebound once the pandemic is over. This option is especially attractive if your property is located near one or more popular tourist destinations.

Buy and Hold

This option involves purchasing a property and holding it over the long term while you wait for its value to grow. Once it has increased significantly in value, you then sell it and make your profit. As you wait for the value of the property to grow, you can still rent it out to tenants to generate some cash flow from it.

House Flipping

House flipping is more of a business than an investment. House flipping involves finding underpriced properties (with some probably being in need of some repairs), renovating the house, making some improvements to increase its value, then selling it at a profit. House flipping involves a huge element of risk since the necessary repairs and improvements can easily end up costing you more than you expected. However, done right, it can generate huge profits quickly. To profit from house flipping, you need to have a keen eye for a property's potential value, be good at locating such underpriced houses, and be knowledgeable about house renovations.

Although you do have all these different options when it comes to investing in real estate, the best approach for someone who wants to build wealth and attain financial freedom is to start off with residential real estate rentals. There are several reasons why investing in residential real estate is more preferable for new investors. These include:

- **Cash flow:** Investing in residential rental properties allows you to generate cash flow from the property while also benefiting from capital appreciation. This is much riskier compared to options such as flipping.

- **Larger tenant pool**: Residential real estate has more demand compared to other types of real estate because everyone needs a place to live. With commercial real estate, you have a smaller pool of renters, which increases the likelihood of the property sitting vacant for extended periods.

• **They perform better during economic crises:** Following the COVID-19 pandemic, lots of businesses have been unable to cover business costs, including rent for business premises. This has caused many businesses to shut down and relinquish their business premises. With residential housing, on the other hand, demand will remain up, even during periods of economic crisis, because people still need a place to stay.

• **They are more affordable:** Residential properties are a lot cheaper compared to commercial properties. Therefore, as a first-time investor who may not have millions of dollars saved up, it is a lot more affordable to invest in residential property. In addition, getting financing for a residential property is a lot easier compared to a commercial property.

• **Tax benefits:** Residential properties offer greater tax benefits compared to commercial properties.

• **Easier to manage:** With residential properties, you are dealing with a relatively low number of tenants, which makes them easier to manage. You can actually manage your residential property by yourself, which can be quite a challenge for a commercial property.

Owing to the suitability of investing in residential rental properties for a first-time investor is what I will be focusing on majorly for the rest of the book. In the next chapter, I will cover the process of choosing a property to invest in.

CHAPTER THREE: TAKING YOUR PICK: CHOOSING A PROPERTY TO INVEST IN

Now that you are conversant with the basics of real estate investing, this chapter will cover everything you need to know about choosing the perfect property to invest in, including how to find suitable properties to invest in, the kind of properties to look for, and how to crunch the numbers to ensure the property will be profitable.

Before you evaluate a property, you first need to find properties that are on sale, so the following is what we will start with.

Where to Find Rental Properties for Sale

Finding suitable rental properties to invest in can be a bit of a challenge, especially if it is your first time doing so. However, there are a couple of strategies you can use to find rental properties that are on sale. These include:

Searching on Multiple Listing Services (MLS)

Searching on an MLS is one of the most popular and most reliable approaches for finding rental properties to invest in. An MLS is a central database that lists all properties that are on sale within a given area, provided they are being sold by a real estate agent.

It's good to note that MLS is only accessible to registered real estate agents. However, you can still search for houses listed on MLS through sites like Zillow, Realtor.com, Trulia, and Redfin.com. These sites aggregate listings from several multiple service listings and make these listings accessible to the public. To search properties on MLS, simply open one of these sites and search for the kind of property you are interested in. You can search for a property by location, price, number of bedrooms and baths, home type, size of the property, available amenities, and so on.

Once you hit search, these sites will provide you with a list of all available homes within the area that meet your search parameters. For each property that appears in the search results, you will get, in addition to your search details, information such as the property address, improvements, and upgrades made on the property, photos, and details about the owner. Some of these sites will even allow you to take a virtual tour of the property.

Since most properties being sold within a given area are listed on MLS (unless the seller has given specific instructions that the property should not be listed), this is an easy way of identifying properties you can potentially invest in without relying on anyone else. It also gives you lots of properties to choose from, which makes it a lot easier for you to find one that meets your needs and preferences. On the flip side, almost every other investor and homebuyer will also be looking for properties to purchase on MLS, which can drive up demand and end up raising the prices of a property you might be interested in.

Working With a Broker or Real Estate Agent

In the previous section, I mentioned that MLS is only accessible to registered real estate agents. While it is still possible to access the information on MLS through sites like Zillow, Trulia, and Realtor.com, the information on the actual MLS is actually more detailed and up-to-date. In this case, you can opt to work with a real estate agent or broker who can provide you with this more detailed, up-to-date information. Your real estate agent can even create a customized search for you, such that you will be notified every time a property that meets your preferences and search criteria is listed on MLS.

Aside from giving you access to the actual MLS, rather than relying on third party sites, working with a broker or real estate agent also allows you to take advantage of the extensive network they have built over the years. Real estate agents are in contact with other real estate professionals, such as contractors, suppliers, lenders, and home inspectors, who could have information about properties that are on sale. By working with a real estate agent, you can take advantage of their network and find properties that are not even listed on MLS (also known as pocket listings).

Foreclosed Properties from Banks

Another great way of finding great deals on a property is to look for properties that are in foreclosure. The great thing about foreclosed houses is that they are often sold below market value, which makes it a lot easier to profit from such properties. In addition, foreclosed properties also come with additional savings, such as lower interest rates, lower down payments, and, sometimes, without the requirement to pay appraisal fees and closing costs.

There are several ways of finding properties that are in foreclosure. The first option is to work with a real estate broker who focuses on foreclosures. Alternatively, you can search for foreclosed properties on sites like Zillow and Trulia. Before a property is foreclosed, banks are legally required to publish a Notice of Sale in local newspapers. By scouring local papers, you can easily find properties that are about to be foreclosed. Most banks will also have on their websites a list of all properties that they have foreclosed. Checking through the websites of major banks in your location can help you to identify foreclosed properties easily.

The foreclosure process is a lengthy one that requires the filing of several legal notices with the County Records Office. Anyone can request access to this information, which means that, by visiting your local records office and searching for Notices of Sale and Notices of Default, you can identify properties that are in foreclosure with relative ease. The best part about this option is that it even allows you to identify properties that are yet to be listed on various foreclosure websites.

Finally, you can find foreclosed properties by driving around neighborhoods you are interested in and looking out for properties with a "Bank Repo" or "Foreclosure" sign. You can get in touch with agents whose contacts are on these signs and enquire about the property in question. These agents can also give you information about other foreclosed properties they may be aware of.

When purchasing foreclosed properties, it is good to note

that these properties are sold on an "as is" basis, which means that you will be responsible for any repairs that need to be made. However, you are not allowed to inspect the properties before purchase, which increases the risk that you could purchase a property with huge and unexpected repair costs. In addition, foreclosed properties could come with delinquencies, such as liens and back taxes, which can increase the costs of acquiring the foreclosed property.

Working with a Wholesaler

Another option for finding great deals on real estate is to work with a real estate wholesaler. These are people and firms who get into contracts with property sellers at a low price, then find buyers to purchase the property at a markup. The best thing about working with a wholesaler is that most wholesalers will give you a professional analysis of a property, including things such as sales and rental comps for similar properties, costs of rehabilitating the property, utility costs, property taxes during sale and rehabilitation, closing costs, insurance costs, demographics of the area, and real estate market trends in the area. Therefore, even for beginners without much knowledge about the real estate industry, it is almost guaranteed that you will be making your investment decision based on correct data and analysis.

In addition, wholesalers help you save time by finding suitable properties for you, charging lower fees than individual real estate agents and brokers, referring you to lenders and other real estate professionals, and, finally, due to their large trade volume, making it a lot easier for you to find properties before they get on the open market.

Driving for Dollars

Lastly, you can find suitable properties to invest in by driving around locations and neighborhoods you are interested in and looking out for properties that look distressed and abandoned. Generally, you should look out for properties that have weeds and overgrown vegetation around them, overgrown grass on the front yard, mailboxes with uncollected mail, broken windows, paint that is peeling off, a pile-up of newspapers on the front door, notices taped on the doors, and so on.

Once you identify such a property, note down its address and take a few photos of the property, noting its current state and any obvious damages. From there, search for the properties on your local tax assessor's website to learn details about the owner. Armed with this information, you can then reach out and express your interest in purchasing their property.

Criteria for Selecting a Property to Invest In

Now that you know where to find deals for rental properties, let us take a look at the criteria you need to follow when choosing a property to invest in. The aim of having criteria for selecting properties is to ensure you don't end up purchasing a property that will have a hard time turning a profit, or one that will give you endless headaches.

We will go over some things you should keep in mind when choosing a property to invest in within the next few sections.

Type of Property

The first thing you need to do before you start searching for suitable properties is to decide on the kind of property you are interested in purchasing. Are you looking for single-family homes, multi-family properties, condos, or turnkey rental properties?

Single-family homes are usually more affordable, and they generally have a greater potential for capital appreciation. Multi-family properties, on the other hand, are more costly than single-family homes, but they generate more cash flow. Condos, on the other hand, are quite easy and inexpensive to maintain, since the condo association is responsible for external repairs. On the flip side, however, condos have a lower potential for capital appreciation, and their rents are usually much lower. Turnkey apartments are a great option because they are ready for renting out immediately after you purchase them, but they are more expensive and have a low appreciation rate.

Although deciding on what rental property to invest in ultimately lies with you, for a new investor, it is advisable to start with single-family homes. On top of being affordable and having greater potential for capital appreciation, they are also likely to attract better, longer-term tenants, which means you won't have to deal with vacancies now and then.

Location

There is a popular phrase that, when it comes to real estate investing, location is king. This is because the location of a property has a *huge* influence on its performance as an investment. The location will affect how much you will be paying for the property, the amount of rent you will charge, the kind of tenants your property will attract, how much the property will appreciate, and so on. Therefore, you need to make sure that any property you consider investing in is in a good location.

Generally, you should aim for properties that are located in areas that are undergoing gentrification, along with areas that have shown a consistent history of capital growth. If possible, you should also go for properties located in areas that are undervalued compared to the major suburbs around them. When you are just getting started, it is also advisable to start by investing in a property located near where you live, since your knowledge of the area will be more intimate, and you will be more likely to recognize factors that affect the real estate market in that area.

Location is a broad factor, and there are several factors that separate a good location from a poor one. Some factors you should consider in the evaluation of a property's location include:

- **The neighborhood:** The neighborhood in which the property is located will have an effect on the kinds of tenants your property will attract, how much you can charge for rent, and how frequently you will have to deal with vacancies. For instance, if your property is located in a dilapidated neighborhood, it won't matter how good your property is—you won't be able to attract high-end tenants who can pay high rents because such tenants will have reservations about living in that neighborhood.

- **Population growth:** Population affects the demand for rental housing. If the population within an area is growing, it means there will be increased demand for rental housing; therefore, there is a high chance that your property will be occupied quite often. If the population is declining, demand for rental housing will also fall, which means you will have trouble finding tenants for your rental property. In this case, investing in a property within an area with a declining population is not a good idea.

- **Job market:** This one is closely linked to the population. An area with great job prospects will attract lots of people, which will increase the population within the area along with the demand for rental housing. If an area has poor job prospects, people will move away in search of opportunities elsewhere, leading to population decline and decreased demand for rental housing.

When evaluating the job market within an area, you should aim for a town or city with several employers. If most people within an area work for the same company, that company shutting down would cripple the economy of that town and drive down demand for rental housing. You can also search for a town or city on the Bureau of Labor Statistics website to get an idea of the job market within the city. If the job market is not doing well, steer clear of that city or town.

- **Access to public transport:** The closer a property is to public transport, the more convenient it is, thus the more likely it is to attract more tenants. Ideally, you should go for properties that are well served by public bus routes, or those within close proximity to a train or subway station. If you want to know if an area is well served by public transport, leave your car behind and try to access the property you want to purchase using public transportation. If it proves to be a huge inconvenience for you, your tenants will find it equally inconveniencing, and will probably opt for a place that is more accessible by public transport.

- **Crime**: This is another important consideration to keep in mind when evaluating the location where a property is located. Would you want to live in a neighborhood where you have to constantly worry about getting mugged, or coming home to find that your house has been burglarized? No one wants that. Therefore, you will want to invest in a property that is located in a relatively safe neighborhood instead.

Before investing in a property, walk around the neighborhood and get a feel for the security within. Are the doors, windows, and HVAC units burglar proofed? Do you notice any broken windows? Are the homes in the neighborhood run down or abandoned? Visit the local library or police precinct and get the crime statistics for the area. Have a chat with the residents and property managers within the neighborhood and ask them about safety and security in the area. If you have reason to believe that there is poor security within an area, don't invest in a property located in that area.

- **Amenities:** People love the convenience of having various amenities close to where they live; therefore, properties located in areas in close proximity to amenities, like restaurants, shopping malls, schools, hospitals, movie theaters, and gyms, are more likely to attract tenants. If possible, you should even invest in such properties.

- **Future development:** When evaluating an area, don't just consider what is there now, but also future developments that may happen in the area. For instance, if you notice lots of construction within the neighborhood, this is a sign the area is in the process of growing, which makes it a suitable investment location. You should also check with the planning department to confirm the zoning plan for the area and any future developments that could hurt your investment. For instance, if there are plans to put up a manufacturing plant close by within five years, such could make the place less desirable due to all the noise pollution from the plant. Knowing about such development plans in advance can prevent you from investing in a property that will make it difficult to attract tenants in the future.

• **Property taxes:** Property taxes will affect the profitability of your investment, so it's important to take them into consideration before settling on a given location. Before settling on a specific location, have a chat with the local tax office and find out how much you will be expected to pay in property taxes, and if there are any plans to hike the taxes in the near future.

• **Average rent:** This aspect will be a good indicator of what you can charge realistically for your property. If the average rent within the area is too little to cover your expected mortgage payments, operating expenses, taxes, and other costs, you will need to do a more careful analysis of the property to make sure you don't end up with a property that will generate negative cash flow.

• **Vacancy rates:** If an area has a high vacancy rate, this signifies a low demand for rental housing in the area, which may then mean the average rent is also likely to be low while landlords struggle to attract tenants. Ideally, you should avoid areas with high vacancy rates.

• **Natural disasters:** To protect your investment, you will need to get insurance for your rental property. If the area you are considering investing in is prone to natural disasters like flooding and earthquakes, this can drive up your insurance costs and eat into your profits. Therefore, you should avoid investing in properties located in areas that are prone to natural disasters.

Characteristics of the Property

Once you have ascertained that the location you are focusing on makes sound investment sense, it is then time to start looking for suitable properties within that location. Just like with the location, there are some factors that you need to keep in mind to ensure that you don't end up making a poor investment. When deciding on a property to invest in, some of the factors you need to watch out for include:

• **Age and condition of the property:** The age and condition of a property will influence its price, capital appreciation potential, maintenance costs, and so on. If you go for a new property, the potential savings from capital depreciation deductions will be higher, and you won't have to spend a lot on maintenance. However, a new property will be much more expensive than an old one. If you don't have lots of money to get started with, you can go for an older property, but you may have to spend more on maintenance. In addition, potential savings from capital depreciation will be much lower. If you decide to go for an older property, it is advisable to hire a home inspector and a contractor to help you determine the repairs that need to be done on the property, and how much they will cost you.

- **Floor plan functionality:** The more functional a property's floor plan is, the easier it becomes to find tenants for the property. When evaluating the functionality of a property's floor plan, check for things such as room spaciousness, separate kitchen, and dining areas, sizable wash areas, adequate natural lighting, and built-in wardrobes.

- **Uniqueness:** Properties with some unique value tend to attract more potential tenants compared to properties that look like a copy of every other property within the neighborhood. However, you shouldn't go for unique attributes that do not add value to the property.

- **Finishes and inclusions:** Properties with high-quality finishes and inclusions—such as stainless steel appliances, wooden floors, and granite benchtops—will attract more tenants compared to properties with normal, average finishes. However, such finishes and inclusions will also drive up property value, meaning you will pay a higher price for it.

- **Title type and zoning:** Before purchasing a property, check the title under which it is registered and the obligations that come with that kind of title. You should also check the zoning of the property lot and the parcels around the property. Consult the local planning department and confirm whether there are any plans to rezone the area, and how these plans will affect property value for the place you're interested in.

- **Construction type:** The type of material a property has been constructed with will have an impact on its maintenance expenses. For instance, you will spend less on maintenance costs for a property constructed using brick compared to one with weatherboard or fibro.

The Importance of Due Diligence

Before making the decision to purchase a property, it is important to make sure you have done all your due diligence to minimize your risk as much as possible. To make it easier for you to conduct your due diligence for any property you are considering investing in, it is advisable that you build around you a team of real estate experts and professionals. Their expertise will be useful when making the decision to purchase a property.

Before paying for a property, consult your team, which should consist of a real estate agent, home inspector, insurance agent, appraiser, real estate attorney, and so on. Your real estate agent will help you find good property deals, your appraiser and home inspector will help you determine whether you are paying the right price for the property and whether the property is in good condition, your insurance agent will help you to figure out insurance costs, and your real estate attorney will make sure all your legal ducks are in order before you make your investment.

Before purchasing a property, make sure you have gotten an inspection of the property, and, with your attorney, check the property's legal status and ensure the property does not have any encumbrances and that the seller has met all their financial obligations. Finally, don't sign any document without consulting your lawyer.

How to Figure Out if the Price of a Property Is Acceptable

Often, sellers will list their properties at a higher price than they expect to fetch for the property. If you want to avoid paying more for a property than it's worth, you will need a way to determine if the price being asked is worth it, or if the seller is charging more than the worth. Knowing how to estimate the value of a property will also help you determine the amount of money you should offer. In the next couple of sections, we will be looking at some tips that will help you estimate the value of any property you are interested in.

The 1% Rule

When purchasing a rental property, you don't want to end up paying too high for a property that doesn't generate enough cash flow. The 1% rule is a formula that real estate investors use to determine whether the cash flow generated by a property is worth the amount they are paying. The 1% rule states that the total monthly rent generated by your residential property should equal or exceed 1% of the purchase price of the property. For example, if the purchase price of a property is $150,000, then the property should be able to generate no less than $1,500 in monthly rent.

Of course, it's impossible to follow this rule to the letter because the ratio of the monthly rent to the value of a property will vary from one location to another. If the property is in a good location with high prospects of growth, you can still invest in the property, even if it is a few points shy of the 1% rule. However, if the ratio of rent to purchase value is *way* below 1%, there is a high chance you are getting a raw deal; in this case, it is advisable that you avoid such a deal or conduct a more detailed analysis of the property before putting down your money.

15% Cash on Cash ROI

While the 1% rule can help you estimate whether the rental income generated by a property makes sense against the price you are paying for the property, it doesn't help you figure out if you will actually generate positive cash flow from that property. A property could meet the 1% rule, but if it has exceptionally high maintenance costs, such could eat into all the money generated from rental income.

To make sure that a property will generate positive cash flow, you need to ensure the property will bring in at least 15% cash on cash ROI. To calculate the cash on cash ROI, estimate the annual cash flow from the property (rent minus expenses), and divide it by the annual debt payments. If the cash on cash ROI is less than 15%, the property won't give you good enough value for your money.

Talk with Your Agent or Appraiser

You can also consult your real estate agent or appraiser to help determine whether the price the seller is asking for is reasonable. These professionals have good knowledge of average property prices within that market and will quickly notice when a seller is charging too much for their property. Ideally, you should go for properties that are selling for below market value, so the value of the property will still remain within the market value after you incorporate things like repairs costs.

Computing the Expenses Associated with a Property

Before putting your money down on a property, you also need to be aware of the expenses associated with the project, since they will have a significant impact on the total amount you will be spending on a property, along with the property's profitability. Some things to keep in mind when calculating the expenses associated with a property include the points we will be going over in the following sections.

Necessary Renovations

Unless you are purchasing a turnkey property, you will probably need to do some renovations and repairs on the property before you can start renting it out to tenants. Before you make the commitment to purchase a property, have your home inspector or contractor inspect the house for you, and identify any necessary repairs and renovations that will be required, along with their costs.

To avoid paying too much for a property and spending even more on repairs and renovations, you should follow the 70% rule. According to this rule, the price you pay to purchase a property should not exceed 70% of the property's after-repair value, minus the repair costs. For instance, let's say that you have identified a property that needs repairs worth $20,000. Once the repairs are done, the market value of the property will be $100,000. In this case, the maximum amount you should pay for the property is 70% of $100,000 (after repair value) minus $20,000 (repair costs). Therefore, the most you should pay for this property is $50,000.

Regular Repairs and Maintenance

Operating a rental property also comes with some regular maintenance costs, such as small routine repairs and utilities, such as power, internet, cable TV, and water. Many new investors forget to take this into account, only to realize later that these costs eat into most of the rental income generated by their property, leaving them with minimal profits. When estimating the maintenance costs, it is good to note that the condition of the property will have an effect on your maintenance costs. For instance, an old property will require more routine maintenance than a newer one, which translates to higher maintenance costs. The kind of tenants renting your property also has an impact on maintenance costs. For instance, a property rented out to college students could be subjected to more damage than one that has been rented out to seniors, so the property with student tenants will likely have higher maintenance costs.

Mortgage Payments

If you used debt to finance your property, you will also need to account for the monthly debt payments as part of your expenses. Monthly mortgage payments will depend on the size of your loan and interest charged by your lender. A huge loan amount, coupled with high-interest rates, will translate to higher monthly payments.

Insurance Payments

Don't forget that you will also need to insure your investment property against risks, such as fire; damage to the property, fixtures, and appliances; and loss of rental income. The insurance costs will vary depending on your property, your insurer, and the risks covered by your policy. Talk to your insurance agent/broker and find out the costs associated with insuring the property before you make your purchase.

Property Taxes

You also need to figure out the amounts you will have to pay in property taxes. Once again, consult the local tax asses-

sor's office to get a good idea of local property tax obligations. It's also good to note that, once you purchase a
property, it will be valued afresh. If the value of the property
has gone up, taxes will also go up. Therefore, when estimating taxes for the property, calculate them based on the
purchase price rather than the property's current assessed
value.

Homeowners Association Fees

Depending on the type of property you are investing
in, as well as the neighborhood where the property is
located, you may also be required to pay a monthly homeowners association fee. These fees go toward the maintenance and improvement of communal areas. Homeowners
association fees are especially common with condos, where
they are used to cover the maintenance costs of common
areas such as elevators, patios, lobbies, and landscaping, as
well as common utilities. Single-family homes with
communal amenities such as swimming pools, tennis
courts, basketball courts, neighborhood parks, and club-
houses might also charge homeowners association fees to
maintain them. It is important to find out if these fees
apply for the property you are investing in and account
for them.

Property Management Fees

If you plan to hire a property manager to manage your
property for you, you will also need to take into account the
fees you will be paying them. Property management fees will
typically cost you between 5-10% of your monthly gross
rental income. Even if you don't intend to hire a property
manager, it is good to account for property management fees

to ensure your property will still be profitable in the event that you decide to bring on a property manager.

Like I mentioned earlier, most beginner investors underestimate the costs and expenses associated with operating their property, only to later realize that these costs are eating into most of their rental income, leaving them with little to no profits.

The best way to avoid underestimating operating costs is to ask the seller to furnish you with a document known as the T12 (document will vary depending on the country you live in). This document contains a record of the total annual income and expenses of a property. Going through this document will help you get an accurate account of all the operating expenses you should expect once you purchase a property.

Sometimes, however, property owners who were managing their property by themselves might not have a T12. In this case, you should ask them to furnish you with all the receipts for utility bills, repairs, and taxes. Going through these receipts carefully will help you determine the expenses associated with operating the property.

Sometimes, you might need to make a quick estimate of the expenses associated with operating a rental property without access to a T12 or receipts. In this case, your best approach is to use the 50% rule. According to the 50% rule, you should make the assumption that you will be spending 50% of your rental income on operating expenses, without taking into account your debt payments. In other words, the cash flow from your property will be equal to 50% of your rental income minus your debt payments. For instance, if you expect a property to bring in $5000 in rental income every month, you should assume that operating expenses will consume $2500. You will then need to pay your mortgage payments from the remaining $2500. Whatever remains, after making your mortgage payments, is your profit. The 50% rule protects investors from underestimating the costs of operating a rental property.

Computing the Profitability of a Property

Now that you have established that the price of a property is reasonable, and having established the expenses associated with operating your property, the last thing you need to do is compute the profitability of the property you want to invest in. To calculate profitability, you will be using the following metrics:

- **Net income:** Net income, also known as net operating income, helps you determine the money that your property will bring in after you have accounted for the monthly expenses of operating the property. However, net income does not take into account your debt payments. To calculate your net income, you should deduct your operating expenses from the total rental income.

- **Cash flow:** Cash flow allows you to determine the money your property brings in after you have covered your operation costs and made your debt repayments. In other words, cash flow is your profit. To calculate cash flow, you should deduct your monthly mortgage payments from net income. If you paid for the property in cash, cash flow will be equivalent to net income.

- **Return on investment (ROI):** The return on investment is a metric that tells you how much profit you are making from your investment property in comparison to the amount of money you put into the investment. Return on investment can be measured in the following three ways:

• **Cap rate:** Cap rate tells you how much money your property is generating against your investment amount, without taking into account your debt payment. To calculate the cap rate, divide your annual net income by the amount you paid for the property. Ideally, you should go for properties with a cap rate of between 8-12%.

• **Cash on cash return:** This metric tells you how much profit your property is generating vis-à-vis the money you have actually put into the property, taking into account your debt payments. Cash on cash return is derived by dividing your annual profit by your annual loan payments. Ideally, you should only invest in properties with a cash on cash return of 10% or more.

• **The total return on investment:** This metric measures the total returns from your property in comparison to the money you have actually put into it. Total annual returns are calculated by adding the annual cash flow from the property to the equity gained, annual capital appreciation, and any money gained in taxes. The total return on investment is calculated by dividing the total annual returns by your annual loan payments.

Once you have evaluated a property you are interested in using the criteria covered in this chapter, determine whether the price is reasonable, taking into account the expenses, and computed the potential profitability of the property, you are then in a good position to determine whether investing in the property makes financial sense. However, don't be quick to pay the price the seller is asking for. Try to negotiate for as low a price as you can. You can also check with rent control regulations in the town or city to figure out if you can increase your profitability by raising the rent.

If the property is suitable, and if the numbers check out, it's time to get ready to purchase the property. For you to do that, you need to get your financing in order, which is what we will be covering in the next chapter.

CHAPTER FOUR: ALL ABOUT THE MONEY: FUNDING YOUR INVESTMENTS

S o far, so good. You now know how to scout for good property deals, select suitable properties to invest in, and crunch the numbers to determine whether a property will be profitable. Now, all you need to do is to get your financing in order, and you will be ready to invest in your first rental property. In this chapter, we will cover the different financing strategies that you can use to finance your investment.

One thing that keeps most people from investing in real estate is how most assume that you need to have millions of dollars saved up before you can invest in property. However, as you will see in this chapter, there are lots of creative financing options that make investing in real estate an affordable venture for most people, even if you don't have tons of money saved up. From these, you can pick an option that works best for you. Some options you can use to finance your real estate investment include what we will be discussing in the following sections.

Using Your Own Cash

Your first option when it comes to purchasing an investment property is to finance it using your own money without having to take on debt. The good thing with using your own cash to finance your investment is that it is quite easy and convenient. You don't have to worry about your credit score or about being approved by a lender.

The problem with this approach is that most beginner investors don't have enough money saved up to cover the full cost of purchasing a property. As a result, this option is not really available for most entry-level investors. In addition, using your own cash to finance a property doesn't offer the best rate of return. It is far better to use the money as a down payment for multiple properties and generate more cash flow, rather than paying for one property to avoid taking on debt.

Conventional Mortgage

This is the most popular option for financing real estate investments. They are typically given by banks and other private lenders. One thing to note about conventional mortgages is that they are not guaranteed by the federal government; therefore, lenders consider them to be very risky. Lenders will likely require you to pay a down payment of between 20-35% to qualify for a conventional mortgage. The lender will also take into consideration your credit score and your credit history before approving you for a mortgage.

Your credit rating will also determine the interest rates you will be getting with the mortgage. In some countries, conventional mortgages come with fixed interest rates. Owing to the large down payment; however, the monthly payments for conventional mortgages are usually lower compared to other types of housing loans.

Another notable thing about conventional mortgages is that they don't take into consideration the expected income from your rental property when approving you for the loan. Therefore, you will need to show proof that you can afford to service the mortgage, even without the future rental income.

Federal Housing Administration Loans

Also referred to as FHA loans, these are housing loans guaranteed by the Federal Housing Administration. The objective behind FHA loans is to make it easier for people without high incomes to own homes. As a result, FHA loans' qualification requirements aren't that stringent. They also require low down payments (about 3.5% in some countries and 5% in others), and they offer low-interest rates. In addition, you can even get a co-borrower for an FHA loan. However, the monthly payments for FHA loans are usually high due to the small down payment. You will also be expected to acquire private mortgage insurance for your FHA loan, which will make your monthly payments even higher.

Since the objective of FHA loans is to help Americans with low incomes purchase their own homes, FHA loans require the person to reside in the property already if they want to qualify for the loan. In other words, FHA loans are not meant to be used to finance investment properties. Despite its normal usage, you can still get around this by purchasing a multifamily home using an FHA loan and living in one of the units while you rent out the others.

Asset-Based Loans

Asset-based loans are a great alternative to conventional mortgages when it comes to financing properties for investment purposes. As you may have guessed from the name, these loans are issued based on the strength of an underlying asset. In other words, to qualify for this kind of loan, it's the asset you are providing as collateral for the loan that matters most, rather than your income level, personal debts, and so on. To qualify for an asset-based loan, you must show that the underlying asset generates enough cash flow to cover the monthly loan payments comfortably. The best part about asset-based loans is that, even if you do not currently own any income-generating asset, you can use the property you are purchasing as collateral for the loan.

Tapping Into Home Equity

If you have built enough equity in your primary home, you can tap into this equity to help you finance the rental property you want to invest in. Equity refers to the difference between the value of your primary home and your remaining mortgage balance. The more you pay off the mortgage, the more equity you build in your primary home. Once you have built sufficient equity, you can then use it as collateral to borrow another loan, which you can then use to purchase a rental property. Most banks will allow you to borrow loans worth up to 90% of your home equity.

Since you are using your home equity as security for the loan, home equity loans do not have tough qualification requirements. However, you will still need to show that you are capable of paying back the loan. In addition, home equity loans usually have relatively low-interest rates, and some may even offer some tax benefits.

There are three ways of tapping into your home equity to help you finance the rental property you want to invest in. The first one is by taking a home equity loan, where you would receive the loan in a lump sum. The loan will be repaid in monthly installments, and, in most cases, the interest rates for the loan are fixed.

The second option is a home equity line of credit, also referred to as a HELOC. Unlike the home equity loan, which comes in a lump sum, a HELOC gives you a revolving line of credit, just like a credit card. You can draw as little or as much as you need from the HELOC, provided it is within the limits of the HELOC. Since it is a revolving line of credit, a HELOC does not come with a fixed interest rate. HELOCs are a great option for raising funds to use as a down payment for a rental property.

The final option is known as a cash-out refinance. With this option, you are essentially taking a new loan on your home. With the money from this loan, you would then repay the remaining balance from the initial loan and have some money left over, which you can then use to finance a rental property for investment purposes.

While tapping into your home equity to finance your investment property is easy and convenient, it has one major disadvantage. The loan is secured by your home, which means that, if you are unable to pay the loan, you could easily end up losing your primary home.

Second Home Financing

If you already own a primary residence, you can take a loan for a second home and use it to purchase another property. One thing to note about second home financing, however, is that you will need to live in this home for some part of the year. Therefore, this option will not work if you intend to rent out the property full-time. In addition, the second home needs to be a certain distance from your primary home. However, it can be a great option for purchasing a property that you can use as a vacation rental.

The good thing about second home loans is that they usually have less stringent qualification requirements, require lower down payments, and offer lower interest rates.

Lease Options: Rent to Own

This is a creative property financing option where you get into a legal agreement with a property owner to lease the property and sublet it to tenants, with the option to purchase the property before the expiry of your lease. If your agreement has a rent to own option, the rent you pay to the owner goes toward clearing the purchase price of the property. At the end of the lease, or at any point before the end of the lease, you can exercise the buy option, in which case, you would only pay the remaining amount from the initial purchase price. It is good to note that, with a lease option, you are under no obligation to purchase the property at the end of your lease period.

The lease option basically allows you to lock the price of a property and make the payments over a certain period. By subletting the property, you can also continue generating an income from it during that period. However, this can be a bit difficult, since the rental payments with a lease option might be higher than average. You will also need to pay the owner upfront in exchange for the option to buy.

The advantage of a lease option is that it doesn't require you to invest tons of cash. You would only pay the option fee, which can be as little as $10, rather than a 20-35% deposit. In addition, you don't need to take on any debt. By subletting the property, you will still be making money, and in case the property appreciates in value, you can purchase it and unlock instant equity.

Mortgage Assumption

Mortgage assumption refers to the process of taking over a mortgage from someone who might be distressed and unable to pay off their mortgage while maintaining the terms. Once the assumption is done, the liability for the loan is transferred to you, and you take over the monthly mortgage payments.

To understand how mortgage assumption works, let's assume that someone took a $200,000 mortgage to purchase a property. After paying off $50,000, they are unable to continue repaying the mortgage, so they decide to sell the property and repay the mortgage. Instead of taking your own mortgage to purchase the property, you can pay $50,000 to the buyer and assume their mortgage. This way, the property, as well as the liabilities of the mortgage, are transferred to you. You become the new owner and pay the remaining $150,000 to the lender in the agreed installments.

The advantage of a mortgage assumption is that it allows you to maintain the terms of the mortgage instead of negotiating new terms for a new mortgage. For instance, if the mortgage was issued at a time when interest rates were lower, you can take over the mortgage and pay lower interest, rather than taking a new mortgage at the higher interest rates being charged currently. In addition, assuming a mortgage is a lot easier than applying for a new mortgage.

It is good to note that not all types of mortgages are assumable. Only loans insured by the U.S. Department of Veteran Affairs and the FHA can be assumed. Even then, you will need to contact the lender to learn the details of the assumption. For instance, some lenders might still ask you to pay a down payment, even when assuming a mortgage. However, the down payments for mortgage assumptions are usually very low.

Borrow from a Peer-To-Peer Lending Network

The Peer-to-peer (P2P) lending network is a relatively new platform that brings together lenders and borrowers. The lenders, in this case, are individuals rather than institutions. The platforms crowdsource funds, which are then given to investors at an interest. The beauty of using P2P lending networks is that their qualifications requirements are a lot less stringent than those of banks and other lending institutions. In addition, loans from lending networks are approved a lot faster, and the interest rates are significantly lower than those of banks and other lending institutions. There are several P2P real estate lending networks you can borrow from, such as Groundfloor, Patch of Land, Lending Home, BitofProperty, and CrowdEstate. The major downside to P2P lending networks, however, is that their repayment periods are usually short.

House Hacking

This is a hack that allows an investor to borrow a loan for a primary residence. By borrowing to purchase a primary residence, you can take advantage of loans with lower qualification requirements and down payments, such as FHA loans. Instead of purchasing a single-family home, you would purchase a multifamily property, such as a duplex or a triplex. Then, you would live in one of the units while renting out the others. Doing so allows you to kill several birds with one stone. It provides you with a house to live in without having to worry about rent, rental income to cover the mortgage payments, and, depending on the property, it might even generate some profit for you to live on, which can definitely kickstart your journey to financial freedom.

Bring in an Investment Partner

If you don't want to take on debt to finance your real estate investment, you can also consider bringing in an investment partner who has enough money to finance the purchase of the property in exchange for equity. However, since your partner is providing the money, you will need to offer some other kind of value, such as providing property management services, bringing in your knowledge of the industry, or scouting for the right deals. Without providing any value, the other person will have no incentive for entering into a partnership with you. If you decide to bring in a partner, you should set out the terms of the partnership from the get-go, so you don't end up getting the short end of the stick or even getting kicked off from the investment. Agree on the roles for each partner, revenue sharing arrangements, the decision-making process, and so on. You can even get creative and make an agreement where you will remit your share of the profits to your partner in exchange for greater equity in the property until you eventually become equal partners in the investment.

From the above information, you can clearly see that there is no shortage of options when it comes to financing your rental property and becoming a landlord. You just need to find one that works for you.

Before ending this chapter, I want to make a disclaimer. Although debt makes it possible for entry-level investors without tons of money saved up to invest in real estate, debt can also be very dangerous. For instance, taking debt to purchase a property that doesn't generate enough rental income to cover operating and mortgage costs can leave you in a worse financial position than where you started. In addition, some other forms of debt, such as home equity financing, can easily leave you homeless should something go wrong. Therefore, you should always be very careful when it comes to using debt to finance your investment property.

Some measures you can take to mitigate risk when using debt to finance your investment property include evaluating properties carefully and making sure you only invest in quality assets, your financing costs are below the cap rate of the property, going for debts with fixed interest rates and fixed payments, and maintaining a high debt coverage ratio. In addition, you should always have enough cash set aside to cover any emergencies and unexpected expenses that may come up. Ideally, your cash reserves should be able to service the mortgage payments and other expenses, such as insurance costs, for a period of about six months. Finally, if possible, you should try and clear your debt as early as you can.

If you keep this in mind, you can easily leverage debt to invest in a rental property and build a foundation for your real estate empire.

In the next chapter, I will cover everything you need to know about renting out and managing your property.

CHAPTER FIVE: GETTING INTO THE THICK OF IT: RENTING OUT AND MANAGING YOUR RENTAL PROPERTY

Having put your financing in order and purchased your first rental property, it is now time to start making money. In this chapter, we will cover everything you need to know about renting out your property to tenants and managing the property to ensure it generates the cash flow you calculated before investing in the property.

Preparing Your Home for Renters

Before you start looking for tenants, you will first need to make sure your property is in good condition and ready for tenants. The condition of your property will determine the ease with which you can attract tenants.

There are several things you need to do to make your property ready for renters. If the property was in need of repairs or renovations when you purchased it, hire a contractor or a rehabber to make these repairs. During the repair phase, you should also check the condition of appliances and fixtures, such as water heaters, HVAC systems, lights, plumbing, fans, and electrical and wiring systems. If any of these are faulty, have them repaired or replaced. You should also ask your contractor to put a fresh coat of paint on the walls.

Once these repairs have been completed, the next thing you need to do is clean the property thoroughly. Have the windows, cupboards, and wardrobes cleaned, find a professional to steam clean the carpets, and have the property sprayed for pests. If the plants in the yard are dead or wilted, replace them. You want your property to look as good as possible. Finally, if you have any valuables in the property, move them to a safer location.

Finding Tenants for Your Property

Now that you have spruced up your property and gotten it ready for tenants, it is time to start advertising your property to potential tenants. Once again, you have several options available to you when it comes to advertising your rental property.

The simplest and one of the most reliable ways of advertising a rental property is to use "for rent" signs. In most cases, people will walk or drive around neighborhoods they are interested in when looking for vacant properties, so putting up "for rent" signs on a window or in the yard is a great way to alert these people that you have vacant units. It's good to note, however, that there are local government and community ordinance regulations on the use and placement of signs; therefore, you should conduct some research first to find out if there are any restrictions on the use of signs in your neighborhood.

Another great option is to advertise your rental property on property advertising websites such as Trulia, RadPad, Hotpads, Apartments.com, Zillow Rental Manager, Rentals.-

com, and Kijiji. The beauty of advertising on these websites is that it is relatively low cost and allows you to get your rental property in front of a wide audience of interested renters. Aside from these websites, you can also advertise your property on Craigslist.

When advertising your property on these sites, you will be competing with other landlords, so you need to make sure your ad is well-crafted. If possible, you can even create a virtual tour of your property and embed it in your ad to show potential tenants what your property looks like, even before they come to look at it.

Today, most people look for everything they need on social media, so advertising your rental property on social media is another great way of finding tenants for your property. There are several Facebook groups geared toward helping people find rental properties in specific towns and cities. You just need to find such groups in your city and advertise your rental property there.

You can also find tenants for your property by partnering with a realtor. The realtor would take up the responsibility of marketing and advertising your property, allowing you to put more focus on managing your property.

Finally, you can also find tenants using the good old word of mouth. Talk to your family and friends and ask them to spread the word for anyone who might be looking for a place to rent about your vacant units. You can even give them an incentive, such as a finder's fee, for every person they refer who ends up becoming a tenant.

Choosing the Right Tenants

Once you start advertising your rental property, you will also start receiving inquiries from potential renters. However, you should not rent out your units to just anyone who is interested. You should screen potential tenants carefully to ensure that you only rent out your property to good people. Good tenants pay their rent on time, keep the property well-maintained, don't disturb their neighbors, among other good behaviors. Bad tenants, on the other hand, will often be late in paying their rent, are a nuisance to their neighbors, may cause damage and destruction to your property, and so on. Bad tenants can turn being a landlord into a major headache for you, so you should try as much as possible to avoid such tenants.

When screening a tenant, there are a couple things you should look at to determine whether to rent out your property to them or not.

The Tenant's Finances

Before renting out your property to someone, you will want to be sure they can actually afford the rent, and the best way to confirm that is to check their source of income. First, you will need to make sure the tenant has a reliable source of income. A regular income reduces the likelihood of the client asking you for more time while they try to raise money for rent. To confirm whether they have a regular income, ask them to provide copies of their bank statements, pay stubs, or tax returns.

Second, you will need to make sure their income is enough to cover their cost of rent and living expenses comfortably. Ideally, the tenant's income should be equal to or more than three times the amount you charge for rent.

The Tenant's Credit

The second thing you need to check is the potential tenant's credit history. This will help you determine whether you can rely on them to pay their rent on time. If the tenant has a history of missed and late payments, this could be an indicator that they will also not pay their rent on time. Similarly, if the tenant has a history of bankruptcies, this is an indicator that they could have problems paying rent on time.

You should also check the amount of credit that the tenant is carrying, as well as their debt to income ratio. A tenant might have a high enough income to afford the rent you are charging, but if they have lots of debt, their debt payments could eat into much of their income, making it difficult for them to pay rent.

The Tenant's Criminal Background

You probably don't want to rent out your property to a convicted criminal. Such a person could be a risk, both to you and your property, as well as the other people renting. Therefore, before renting out your property to someone, you will need to run a criminal background check. Make sure you notify them and have them sign a form to that effect. While minor misdemeanors should not keep you from allowing someone to live on your property, you may want to reconsider if you find out that they have a serious criminal record. You should also keep yourself aware of state laws surrounding discrimination of people with criminal records, so you don't end up on the wrong side of a lawsuit.

The Tenant's Stability

Every time your rental units sit vacant, you are missing out on the rental income from those units. In addition, finding a new tenant for the vacant units comes with its own cost. Therefore, it is important that you, as a landlord, find tenants who are likely to rent your property for the long term. One major factor that affects a tenant's likelihood of living in your property for the long term is their stability. How stable is their job? How often have they changed jobs in the last two or three years? How often have they moved in the last two or three years? If you notice a potential tenant doesn't seem to be in a stable situation, it may be wise to pass them over because there is a high chance that such a tenant will only stay in your property for a few months.

The Tenant's Rental History

Finally, before renting out your property to someone, it is important to find out the kind of relationship this person has had with their former landlords. Before renting out to a potential tenant, ask them to furnish you with the contacts of two or three of their previous landlords. Reach out to the landlords and ask about the tenant. Do the landlords think they were a good tenant? Were they ever late with their rent payments? Did the landlord evict them, or did they move out on their own volition? Did they give a notice before moving out? Asking these simple questions can help you determine whether the tenant will be giving you headaches or not.

Considerations for Your Lease

After screening and approving a tenant, the final thing you need to do before allowing them to move into your property is to ask them to sign a lease agreement. The lease agreement sets out the conditions for renting and your expectations from the tenant for the duration that they will occupy the property. Below are some things you should include in your lease contract:

- The tenant's names and contact information.

• The duration of the lease. Once this period expires, the tenant can either move out or renew the contract.

• The rent amount for renting the property and the procedure for making rent payments.

• The latest date by which the tenant should have paid their rent and the consequences for late payment.

• The amount of deposit that the tenant will need to pay before moving in and any other applicable fees.

• How issues surrounding repairs and maintenance should be handled, including the procedure for making repair requests and responsibilities of both parties, as it pertains to repairs and maintenance.

• Regulations and restrictions about keeping pets within the property.

• Whether you, as the landlord, has the right to enter the property for inspection and the amount of notice you should provide if you intend to do so.

• Parking instructions for properties with a provided parking space.

• Regulations around activities that the tenant is prohibited from carrying out within the premises.

• Regulations and restrictions about alterations the tenant can/cannot make to the property.

• The procedure for submitting a notice about the

intention to vacate and your expectations about the condition of the property upon move-out.

• Any other rules and regulations you want the tenant to be aware of before moving in.

When creating your lease agreement, you can also consider offering lease options as a scheme. This is especially good for someone who has plans to exit from their real estate investment. Lease options have a lot of advantages. They allow you to charge higher rent, the tenants will take better care of the property because they are considering purchasing it from you, and it allows you to secure a prearranged sales price for that property.

Once the tenant has signed the lease agreement, you can then allow them to move into the property. Before they move in, however, it is also advisable to take some photos of the property to act as documentation and proof of the property's condition prior to move-in. This will make it easier for you to assess any damage made on the property when the tenant moves out.

Managing Your Property

Now that you have found tenants, it is time to start thinking about how you will manage your property. This is important because it will have an impact on your property's performance and profitability.

When it comes to managing your property, you have two options. The first one is to manage the property by yourself. This means that you would be responsible for everything, including dealing with tenants, handling your taxes, keeping the property maintained, handling or overseeing repairs, dealing with legal issues, keeping records, and so on.

It may not seem like it, but managing your rental property by yourself is not a walk in the park, especially for someone who has no prior experience in the real estate industry. I have seen many entry-level investors try to manage their own properties, only to realize later that it is a lot harder than they anticipated. In addition, if you have another job that occupies most of your time, you will have very little time left to manage your rental property. As a result, I always encourage entry-level beginners to go with the second option, which is hiring someone else to manage the property for you.

Hiring a property manager offers several advantages. First, it allows you to outsource every aspect of managing your property to a professional, which increases the likelihood of your property performing well. In addition, it frees up your time, allowing you to put greater focus into finding great deals and growing your real estate portfolio. Having a professional property manager also means that you won't have to deal with messy legal issues. A professional property manager will most likely have a legal department handle those issues for you. Finally, hiring a professional property manager gives you the confidence that your property is in safe hands when you don't have time to do it yourself, or when your rental property is some distance away from your primary residence, which would have made it difficult for you to manage the property yourself.

Next, we will go over some roles that would be handled by a professional property manager.

Rent Management

A property manager will handle every aspect of rent management, including setting the right amount of rent to maximize profits while keeping your property attractive to tenants, making sure rent is paid on time and enforcing late fees, and adjusting the rent depending on market forces. The property manager will also be responsible for handling deposits and refunds whenever a tenant is moving in or out.

Tenant Management

Your property manager will also be responsible for every aspect of tenant management. This includes advertising and marketing your property to attract tenants, making the property ready for tenants, screening and running background checks, and handling lease agreements, the last point which would include making sure the agreement has all the necessary clauses that would protect all parties and making sure the terms are adhered to.

Additionally, the property manager will deal with issues like tenant complaints, emergencies, and move-outs. They would also deal with evictions for those unable to adhere to the terms in the lease agreement.

Handling Property Maintenance and Repairs

Part of managing a rental property is ensuring the property is in good condition and that it is safe for your tenants. A professional manager will be responsible for the routine maintenance of your rental property, such as making sure the trash is collected, keeping the communal areas clean, tending the yard, shoveling snow during winter, and so on. The property manager will also be responsible for handling any repairs within the property.

Supervisory Responsibilities

In some cases, you might need to hire some staff to

perform various tasks, such as security personnel, a concierge, and a cleaner, for example. It is the responsibility of the property manager to make sure these people do their jobs and they are getting paid for their work. The property manager will also be responsible for keeping an eye on vacant units to make sure they don't get vandalized.

Managing the Budget and Keeping Records

For your rental property to operate profitably, you will need to have a budget for various costs and expenses. A property manager will handle tasks like setting the budget (with your approval, of course) and making sure this budget is adhered to. They will also be responsible for maintaining records of everything about the property, including all income, expenses, lease agreements with tenants, complaints, maintenance requests, and repairs done and their costs.

Taxes

Sometimes, complying with all tax obligations for rental properties can be hectic. A property manager will help you understand your tax obligations, and they can even help you file all the necessary taxes for your property.

Awareness of the Landlord-Tenant Law

If you don't have a good understanding of both federal and local laws and regulations surrounding the landlord-tenant relationship, you can easily find yourself facing lawsuits for something you never considered being wrong. A property manager can help keep you on the right side of the law when dealing with various tenant issues, such as tenant screening, handling of security deposits, lease termination and evictions, and compliance with property safety standards.

You can probably see that hiring a property manager is a lot better than managing the property by yourself. They take away the stress of being a landlord, making your investment even more passive. Of course, even if you decide to hire a property manager, it is still up to you to decide how involved you want them to be, depending on how hands-on you want to be as well. If you want to take on some responsibilities, you can renegotiate the property management fees.

The Importance of Keeping Your Property Well-Maintained

Another important thing you need to do as a landlord is to keep your property well-maintained and in good condition. There are several reasons why you need to do this. First, it is your legal obligation under the landlord-tenant law to make sure your property meets certain health and safety standards, including keeping the place clean and providing somewhere for your tenants to dispose of their waste.

Second, keeping your property well-maintained is a good way of keeping your current tenants and attracting new ones to your property. No one wants to live in a dilapidated property with cracked walls, peeling paint, and leaking pipes.

Keeping your property in good condition also helps you to save money. It is a lot easier to fix minor issues and do minor repairs as they occur. If you leave them unrepaired, they could balloon into bigger problems that will be more costly to repair. In addition, your tenants are more likely to take better care of your property when it is in better condition compared to if it were more run-down. You can also charge higher rent for a property that is in good condition and when everything is working as it should. A well-maintained property will also result in lower utility bills.

Finally, keeping your property well-maintained helps preserve its value and increases the potential for capital appreciation. When you decide to sell your property, it will be easier to find buyers if you have maintained your property properly over the years, and you can then fetch a higher price for it in the future.

Common Problems When Managing a Rental Property

Like I mentioned earlier, managing a rental property is not a walk in the park. It comes with its own set of challenges that you will have to learn to deal with if you want your property to be profitable. Next, let's take a look at some common problems you may encounter when managing a rental property, as well as how to handle them.

High Turnover Rate

As a landlord, one of the worst things you could have to deal with is high turnover rates. High turnover hurts you in two ways. First, it reduces your rental income for the duration that your property sits vacant. Depending on the number of vacant units, your rental income might get so low that you become unable to meet your debt obligations, forcing you to make mortgage payments out of pocket, which is every landlord's nightmare.

Second, a high vacancy rate means you will be on constant lookout for new tenants. This will also cost you money because you have to advertise the vacant units, spend time and money conducting background checks and running the administrative duties, and other costs associated with preparing your property for a new tenant.

Fortunately, there are a number of things you can do to reduce your turnover rate and keep your property in good financial health. First, you should aim to be a good landlord who puts the welfare of your tenants first, which requires communicating with them regularly, quickly responding to their requests, and taking other proactive steps to keep them happy. Another way to reduce turnover is to charge fair rents. If your tenants believe you are charging fair rents for your rental property, they will be less likely to be inclined to move. If, on the other hand, they feel that your rent is exorbitant, it will just be a matter of time before they look for and move to another place where they deem rent costs are fairer.

Keeping your rental property well-maintained is another way of retaining your tenants over the long term. Like I mentioned earlier, no one wants to live in a dilapidated rental. If you want your tenants to stick around, prioritize keeping your property looking good, making necessary repairs on time, and so on.

Finally, you can also reduce your turnover rate by applying proper screening processes before allowing someone to occupy your rental. Go for tenants who have stable jobs, a regular source of income, and a history of staying in one place for a long time. If you rent out your property to tenants with a history of moving every couple months, you can bet they won't stay in your rental for long either.

Late Rent Payments

Another common problem among landlords is late rent payments. Having tenants who do not pay their rent in time can cause a lot of frustrations and make it impossible for you to handle your obligations on time, such as paying for services and utilities and making mortgage payments. If you notice that you constantly have to deal with late payments, you may have to consider being stricter with your rent collection rules, enforcing late payment fees, and/or working with a property manager who will ensure that rents are paid on time. Remember that it is always a good idea to screen tenants carefully, so you can ensure you are only renting out your property to tenants who won't have trouble paying their rent on time.

Staying Organized

As part of being a landlord, you will have to deal with lots of paperwork—lease agreements, rent receipts, payments made to service providers, utility bills, and so on. All this paperwork can easily get overwhelming, leading to lots of stress, and losing some of the paperwork can create huge problems for you.

To avoid this, you need to be proactive in keeping yourself and your paperwork more organized. Strategies include creating a logical filing system, not allowing paperwork to accumulate on your desk, and keeping digital copies of all documents.

Legal Problems

There are several laws and regulations that apply to landlords, and, if you are not aware of them, you can easily find yourself in lots of legal trouble. To avoid this, you will need to keep yourself conversant with all the laws and regulations —federal, state, and local—that apply to landlords. This will not be easy, but it is an absolute *must* if you don't want to find yourself battling legal suits constantly. Alternatively, you can hire a professional property manager who is knowledgeable about all legal matters surrounding the landlord-tenant relationship.

Dealing with Frequent Evictions

Evicting someone from your property is not an easy thing to do. It takes both an emotional and financial toll on you, especially if you have to do it frequently. This is a situation you should try to avoid as much as possible.

There are three steps you can take to reduce the likelihood of having to deal with tenant evictions. The first is to ensure you have a thorough screening process. This way, you will increase the likelihood of renting out your property to tenants who are unlikely to be troublesome. The second step is to create payment plans for tenants who are unable to pay their rent on time. Sometimes, even the most well-meaning tenants may fall onto some hard times. Instead of making a quick decision to evict them, you can come up with a payment plan that can help them clear their arrears. In most cases, this is a better option than evicting them.

The third step is to focus on creating healthy relationships with your tenants. This works for two reasons. First, having a relationship with them will make them feel bad about not paying you on time, and, even when they run into problems, they will find it easy to talk to you rather than avoid you. Second, when you have strong relationships with your tenants, they will be more likely to respect you and your property, which then means they will take better care of your property and will be less likely to disturb their neighbors.

Dealing with Unexpected Expenses

Although most of the repairs you will have to deal with will be minor and won't cost you much, there will be situations when you may find yourself having to deal with an unexpected big-ticket repair, such as a having to replace a roof, the HVAC system, water heater, and so on. Without proper planning, you could be forced to cover such costs from your own pocket.

To avoid this, it is advisable to set aside some reserve cash for such expenses. This way, you won't be caught unawares and your cash flow will not get burned by such expenses. It is also advisable to set aside some cash to cater for the property's expenses during months when it will be sitting vacant.

Handling Your Tax Obligations

Managing a rental property properly also means making sure you are handling your tax obligations properly. The problem here is that tax obligations on rental properties can be quite complicated, which can leave one pretty confused, especially for a first-time landlord. The best approach here is to hire an accountant who is well versed in matters surrounding rental property taxes. Such a professional will ensure you are always in compliance with all your tax obligations.

One of the best things about rental properties is that you are allowed to make several deductions on your tax obligations. Your accountant will definitely help you understand which deductions apply to your property, so let's take a look at some of the most common tax deductions for rental properties.

Depreciation

This is one of the biggest tax deductions for investors with rental properties. Ordinarily, businesses are allowed to deduct the cost of acquiring an asset when filing their tax returns. Since a rental property is like a business, you can take advantage of this to deduct the cost of various assets from your taxes, including the property itself and other assets, such as furniture, appliances, and improvements made to the property.

For something to be treated as a depreciable asset, it needs to be something expected to last for over a year. In other words, it should add some kind of value to your business (in this case, it should add value to your rental property), and it needs to be something that wears out or loses value over time.

It's good to note that, with depreciation, you won't deduct the entire cost of acquiring an asset all at once. Instead, you would deduct a portion of the cost gradually over the lifetime of the asset. Figuring out how to deduct depreciation of an asset can be a bit complicated; therefore, it is best to consult your accountant to have them guide you through this.

The Cost of Repairs

Making repairs to your property is seen as a business expense, so you are allowed to deduct the amount of money spent on repairs in a given year when filing your taxes. Any work done to keep your rental in good working condition is considered as a repair, provided it does not lead to a significant increase in the property's value. For instance, works such as painting the walls or fixing leaking plumbing are considered to be repairs. However, work involved in replacing the roof or adding a new room are seen as improvements rather than repairs because they increase the value of the property. Instead of being deducted as repairs, improvements are treated as assets and are thus depreciated over their lifetime.

Interest

If you took a mortgage to finance your rental property,

the interest paid on the mortgage is considered to be a business expense, which means you are allowed to deduct it from your tax obligations. In addition to interest on your mortgage, you can also deduct interest paid on your credit cards, provided the funds from these credit cards were used for business expense purposes in relation to your rental property.

Travel Expenses

If you engage in any business-related travel as a landlord, both local and long distance, you are allowed to deduct the cost of this travel when filing your taxes. However, this travel needs to be related to your rental property business. For instance, if you live away from your rental property and need to travel regularly to check on your property and deal with some management tasks, you can deduct the costs incurred during these travels. Travel costs will include the cost of gas or transport expenses if using public transport. In addition, you can deduct other related costs, such as interest on your car loan, tolls and parking fees incurred during travel, and even car registration fees if applicable.

Passive Activity Losses

In most cases, investing in rental real estate is considered a passive activity. As a result, investors are allowed to claim passive activity losses on losses incurred from their real estate investment, but up to a certain limit. A passive activity loss can be defined as any financial loss stemming from an investment in which the investor is not actively involved. Passive activity loss is governed by many complex rules, so it is best to consult your accountant and have them advise on how you can take advantage of passive activity losses.

Professional Fees

As a landlord, it may be necessary to work with various professionals, such as an attorney, real estate agent, accountant, home inspector, appraiser, and other professional advisors. Consulting such professionals is considered a business expense; as a result, any fees paid to these professionals are tax-deductible.

Employee Compensation

As a landlord, you may also need to hire some employees to help with the operation of your rental property, such as a property manager, contractor to help fix problems within the property, live-in superintendent, concierge, and so on. These are seen as business expenses; therefore, the wages paid to such employees are tax-deductible.

Property Taxes

Owning a property comes with its own set of taxes known as property taxes. In addition, for a rental property, you may be required to pay other taxes, such as local licensing fees and occupancy taxes. When it comes to filing taxes on income from your rental property, you can deduct the amounts paid in the above property taxes, since they can be termed as business expenses.

Insurance

To operate a rental property, you will need to keep the property insured. You might also need to pay for other types of insurance cover, such as accident insurance, health insurance for your employees, and liability insurance. The premiums paid for these insurance covers are seen as business expenses, meaning you are allowed to deduct them from your taxes.

Other tax-deductible expenses also include advertising costs, telephone calls made as part of running your rental property, and expenses incurred to make your rental accessible to the elderly or people with disabilities.

One thing to note when it comes to claiming deductions on your taxes is that you will be required to provide proof in case the IRS decides to audit your rental property. Therefore, it is very important that you keep accurate and detailed records of all your income from your rental property, along with all expenses incurred during operation. Every claim you make on your taxes should be backed by a relevant document.

Generally, taxes for rental properties can be quite complicated and will vary from one location to another, so it's advisable that you work with a professional accountant to ensure you always meet your tax obligations.

If you follow the tips covered in this chapter, you will find it a lot easier to rent out and manage your rental property, which will, in turn, lead to better performance of your investment and improved profitability. In the next chapter, we will look at how to grow your portfolio and move closer to financial independence, which is your ultimate goal.

CHAPTER SIX: INCHING CLOSER TO FINANCIAL FREEDOM: GROWING YOUR PORTFOLIO

So far, you have learned how to choose properties to invest in, how to finance your investments, and how to rent out and manage your investments to generate cash flow. If you have already done this, congratulations! You now have a rental property generating passive income for you.

The idea behind this book, however, is not simply to help you generate some additional income on the side, but rather to help you achieve financial independence. For that to happen, you have to move beyond generating rental income from just one property—you have to start thinking about expanding your portfolio to where your investments will be generating more money than you need to survive. This means you need to start thinking of your real estate investments as a long-term game rather than a get-rich-quick scheme.

In this chapter, I will provide you with the right tools and strategies to help you grow your portfolio quickly, along with other tips that will help you maximize your returns and achieve your investment goals much faster.

Although I have mentioned that your first rental property will not get you to financial freedom, it is still a crucial step in your journey to financial freedom; one that will have set the stage for your other investments. It is also one of the hardest steps. Additionally, if you talk to most millionaires and billionaires who have made their wealth by investing in the real estate sector, most of them will tell you that purchasing their first property was the most difficult step of their journey to wealth. Once you take this crucial first step, things become a lot easier.

Therefore, although it is important to take your time when picking your first investment property, don't get too caught up with trying to get everything right on the first try. Just like an amateur baseball batter is unlikely to hit a home-run on their first try, you are also unlikely to find a winner with your first deal. All this means it's advisable to start by investing in smaller and cheaper properties. This will allow you to learn the ropes without putting too much money at stake. From there, as you get more experienced in real estate investing, you can then move to even bigger deals. As you continue expanding your portfolio, you should also put a lot of focus on learning. Every single investment you add to your portfolio should be seen as an opportunity to learn more about the real estate industry. This commitment to lifelong learning will play a critical role in helping you achieve financial freedom.

How Many Properties Should You Have in Your Portfolio?

Having said that you cannot achieve financial freedom by investing in one rental property, you might be wondering how many properties you will need in your portfolio to be financially independent. The answer to this question is that... it depends.

In Chapter 1, I asked you to compute how much money you need to live comfortably depending on your lifestyle, preferences, family size, where you live, and so on. This calculation will determine the number of properties you need to have in your portfolio. For instance, if you have determined that you would need $6,000 every month to live comfortably, the properties in your portfolio should be able to generate more than $6,000 in cash flow every month, with all operating expenses and mortgage payments taken care of. Similarly, if you need $10,000 every month, the properties in your portfolio should be able to generate more than $10,000 per month.

For even better results, don't just stop when you feel your investments can then cover your living expenses. Instead, focus on constantly expanding your portfolio of rental properties, such that you can afford anything you want without having to think too much about money. This is what true financial freedom looks like: being able to do whatever you want without having to worry about not having enough money to follow through. So, how do you go about growing your rental property portfolio?

Different Ways to Grow Your Portfolio

If expanding a portfolio of rental properties was easy to do, everyone would have done it. However, in most cases, investors who are interested in growing their portfolio of properties face one major challenge: access to financing. Acquiring financing for one property is already hard enough —getting the financing to purchase multiple properties is a lot more difficult. Fortunately, there are some tactics you can use to grow your portfolio quickly without drowning yourself in debt. Next, let's take a look at three strategies that will help you grow your portfolio until you achieve financial freedom.

The Snowball Method

Snowballs usually start as small, almost insignificant balls. As the ball rolls down the snow-covered hill, however, it starts picking up more snow and gaining mass, which then gives it more momentum as it moves down the hill. Within no time, it would build itself into a huge ball of snow moving at great speeds. Just like a snowball grows in size and momentum as it rolls down the hill, you can also use this concept to expand the size of your rental property portfolio.

Applying the snowball method to real estate investing requires that you save most (or all) of the cash flow from your first investment property and use it to finance your second property, then repeating the same method to finance your third property, and so on. To make this easier to understand, I will be using an illustration.

Let's assume you have one rental property generating $1,000 in cash flow every month. Assuming that you are saving all this money, at the end of the year, you will have $12,000 in savings. Now, assuming that you need a $25,000 down payment to acquire a similar property, this would mean that, if you saved all the cash flow from your first property, you can then afford a new property in just over 2 years. By this point, you will have two rental properties in your portfolio.

Taking into account that the second property is also generating $1,000 in cash flow every month, you will then be gaining $2,000 per month, which also means you will be able to afford your third property in just over a year, rather than the 2 years it took you to afford your second property.

If you repeat the same method with your three properties, your portfolio will then be generating $3,000 every month. This means you can afford the down payment for another property within 9 months, rather than a whole year. Alternatively, you can save the money for a longer time and purchase a bigger property, which will bring in greater cash flow and make it easier for you to afford another property even faster.

Just like a snowball, you can start with a small cash flow and use it to build momentum and acquire more properties. The longer you stick to it, the easier it will become for you to acquire even more properties and expand your portfolio. This is a relatively effective technique for growing a real estate portfolio, and it is no surprise that it is trusted and used by billionaires such as Warren Buffet. For this strategy to work, however, you must make a commitment to save as much of your cash flow as you can. This means you will need another source of income to keep you afloat while you build your snowball. In other words, don't quit your day job just yet—at least not until your snowball builds enough momentum to allow you to use the cash flow from one property to cater to your living expenses without affecting the overall momentum.

The BRRRR Technique

This is another great technique for expanding your portfolio and building wealth. The letters BRRRR stand for Buy, Rehabilitate, Rent, Refinance, and Repeat.

With the BRRRR technique, you would start by finding and *buying* properties that are selling for below market value. Such properties will usually have some issues that need to be fixed; therefore, the second step is to *rehab* the properties and improve their condition. Once you have rehabbed a property, you can then start *renting* it out to tenants to generate some income. Part of this rental income will go into repaying the mortgage for the property. You can also use some of your profits from the property to cover the debt, which will allow you to build equity in the property a lot faster.

Once you have built significant equity, you can then *refinance* the property. Refinancing allows you to pull out your capital from the property. You can then use this capital as a down payment for your second property. This is where the final step comes in: *repeat*. Once again, find another property selling for below market value and repeat the entire process.

As you may have noticed, the BRRRR technique allows you to use the same capital to purchase multiple properties rather than having to save money to put down on each. Of course, building enough equity in a property to refinance will take some time, but you can speed up the process by using the profits from the properties to clear your debt, which will allow you to acquire the next property much faster. Finally, to build a sizable portfolio of rental properties, you will need to repeat this process several times. This is not a get-rich-quick scheme; with time, however, this strategy can help you build a real estate empire.

1031 Exchange

This third strategy allows you to take advantage of section 1031 of the Internal Revenue Code to make the most of your real estate investments and avoid paying capital gains tax. According to section 1031 of the Internal Revenue Code, investors can dispose of their assets without attracting capital gains tax liability from the sale of the asset, provided they acquire another similar asset within a specified time.

So, how would you take advantage of the 1031 exchange to grow your portfolio?

Let's say you are a new investor who has just purchased their first rental property. You rent out the property and start generating cash flow from it. A few years down the line, the property has appreciated in value, and you can sell it for a profit. Ideally, you would be required to pay capital gains tax following the sale, which would have reduced your profits. However, taking advantage of the 1031 exchange, you purchase another property quickly using the proceeds from the sale and avoiding paying any tax on your profits. Since you now have more money (initial capital + profits + capital gains tax savings), you then purchase a bigger and better property that is capable of generating greater cash flow.

A few years later, after generating even more cash flow from your property (which you can use to finance another property), the property has once again appreciated in value, so you sell it and purchase another similar property quickly. Since you have more money by this point, you would then, once again, purchase a bigger and better property that is capable of generating even more cash flow. As you continue with this chain of events, you continue growing your capital without paying any capital gains tax while the cash flow from your portfolio keeps growing.

For you to take advantage of the 1031 exchange, however, there are some conditions that need to be met. First, your acquired property following the sale needs to be equal to or greater in value compared to the property you just sold. Second, the proceeds from the sale should be held by a qualified intermediary who would then transfer them to the seller of the property you want to acquire. Third, you will need to identify the replacement property you want to purchase formally within 45 days of selling the other. Finally, you must complete the purchase of the replacement property within 180 days of selling the other property; otherwise, the 1031 exchange will not apply.

With these three techniques, you can easily and quickly grow your rental property portfolio, even if you don't have millions of dollars to finance the purchase of multiple properties. You just need to find a technique that works for you and use it to expand your portfolio. As a savvy investor, you can even use a combination of these three strategies to supercharge the growth of your rental property portfolio. For instance, you can use the BRRRR technique to pull out your capital from your properties and finance other properties, while also following the snowball technique with the cash flow from your properties to finance even more properties. Once your properties appreciate in value, you can then sell them and take advantage of the 1031 exchange to increase your capital and acquire properties with greater cash flow potential, without having to pay any capital gains tax on the sales.

The Importance of Diversifying Your Real Estate Portfolio

When it comes to investing your money, you have probably heard that you should never put all your money in one basket. This applies to all kinds of investments, including investing in rental real estate. Putting all your money into one investment makes you highly vulnerable because a single downturn can potentially wipe out your entire investment. Therefore, it is important to keep your portfolio diversified; this way, a downturn will only affect a portion of your investment. In other words, portfolio diversification helps you to minimize your risk.

When it comes to rental real estate, there are two major ways to diversify your portfolio.

Investing in Multiple Units

By itself, expanding your portfolio of rental properties is a way of diversifying. Let's imagine your only investment is one single-family home. If your tenant moves out and the property sits vacant for two months, you will have zero cash flow for those two months. If you had three single-family properties, on the other hand, you would still have some cash flow, even if one property was vacant for some time.

While investing in several single-family properties is a form of diversification, the best way to diversify your portfolio of rental properties is to invest in multi-family properties. While single-family properties are good for a first investment, once you start expanding your portfolio, you should go for multi-family properties.

Multi-family properties offer several diversification advantages. First, they help minimize the impact of vacancies. Since you have multiple units within one property, a vacancy in one of the units does not cut off your cash flow. You can still meet your obligations (taxes, mortgage payments, maintenance costs, etc.) and probably still gain a profit from the remaining occupied units. In addition, multi-family units allow you to generate greater cash flow from a single investment. You would only purchase a single property, but it generates more cash flow than you would have generated from a single-family unit of similar value.

Investing in Different Locations

Another great way to diversify your portfolio of rental properties is to invest in properties located in different areas —different suburbs, different cities, or even different states. This is because, in most cases, real estate markets in different locations move independently. Therefore, by investing in properties in different areas, a downturn in one area will not affect your entire portfolio. For instance, let's assume the main employer in a certain town has just closed shop, leading to a downturn in the job market of that town and decrease in demand for rental housing. If all your properties are located in this town, your entire portfolio would be affected. However, if you only had one property in this town and several other properties in other towns and cities, only one property in your portfolio will be affected by this downturn. All this means that you should avoid investing in several properties located within the same location.

Apart from these two options, you can also diversify your income by finding new ways to generate income from your rental property. A good way to do this is to consider offering value-added services, such as installing a vending machine in a common area, installing washers and dryers and charging a fee to use them, offering housekeeping services, adding storage units and charging tenants to use them, investing in additional parking and charging for it, charging pet fees, and so on. This can help you supplement your income from your rental property.

Increase the Value of Your Properties

If you want to increase the returns from your rental property, you can also consider increasing the property's value. Increasing your property's value has several advantages. First, it improves the condition of your property, which makes it easier for you to attract new tenants and retain your current tenants. In addition, improving the condition of your property allows you to charge higher rent, thus increasing the cash flow from the property without a significant increase in investment. Finally, increasing the value of your rental property increases your equity, giving you greater leverage that you can use to finance other properties and expand your portfolio.

There are several methods you can use to add value to your rental property. Some easy things you can do to increase the value of your property include:

• **Make some repairs and improvements**: If you just purchased a rental property that was selling for below market value, there is a high chance the property needs some tender loving care. Making a few inexpensive repairs to such a property can immediately and dramatically increase its value, allowing you to charge higher rents and increasing your equity.

• **Replace the carpets:** Something as small as the condition of the carpets in your property can make the property unattractive, making it a lot harder for you to attract tenants or charge high rent. Therefore, if the carpets on the floors look worn or stained, you should consider replacing them. You will be surprised at the difference such a small change will make. Alternatively, you can consider installing Hardie floorings, such as bamboo, laminate, or wood. Such flooring can make the property look warmer and more elegant, thus increasing its value.

• **Take care of the basics:** Sometimes, all you need to increase the value of your rental property is to take care of the basics; that means, making sure it has been maintained properly, conducting regular checks, making repairs in a timely manner, and making sure the common areas are cleaned regularly.

• **Improve the external appearance of the property:** The external appearance of a property plays a major role in its perceived value, both by tenants and by potential buyers. By improving the external appearance, you can increase the value of your rental property significantly. You can improve the external appearance of your property through inexpensive fixes, like putting a fresh coat of paint on the external walls, making sure the lawn or yard is well-tended, or adding some fresh flowers. The nicer your property looks, the higher its perceived value.

• **Upgrading the fixtures:** Improving fixtures that look old and dingy can also increase the value of a property dramatically. Consider upgrading the plumbing, lighting, and bathroom fixtures, for example. Most of these fixtures are fairly inexpensive, yet the effect of upgrading them will be significant.

• **Go for some added extras:** If you have some money to spend, consider adding some extras, such as top-of-the-line range kitchen appliances, washers, and a good security system. Although such extras may cost you, they will give your property a luxury feel, thereby increasing the property's value and making it more attractive to tenants.

These are just some of the options you can take to increase the value of your property. Take a look at your rental property and think of what you can do to increase its value. Even though some of them may require you to spend a considerable sum of money, you will reap the benefits of this investment through increased demand for your property by potential tenants and increased equity, which you can leverage to finance the purchase of more properties.

Have an Investment Strategy

As you start expanding your portfolio of rental properties, it is good to have an investment strategy in mind. Don't purchase additional properties just for the sake of it. Before investing in any rental property, consider what you want to achieve from the investment and how that ties to your goal of attaining financial independence. Don't make an investment just because someone else made a similar investment; it may have been a good investment for them, but it could be a poor one for you because you both have different goals for your investments.

As you start expanding your portfolio, take the time to think about your long-term goals. Are you just looking to build a portfolio of rental properties that will give the money you need to live comfortably, say $100,000 every month? Otherwise, are you more focused on building equity and leveraging it to make even more investments that will eventually make you a millionaire? Once you have a clear picture of what you want to achieve in the long term, it will become easier for you to choose properties aligned with your goals, and you will waste less time investing in properties that do nothing for you.

Finally, you should know when to cut your losses. Regardless of how careful you are, there is always a chance that you may put your money into an investment that will take money out of your pocket instead of putting it in. Most investors have found themselves in such a situation. The difference between savvy investors and ordinary investors lies in what they do after the fact.

When they realize they have made a poor investment, savvy investors don't hold onto it in hopes that it will turn around someday. They know that the more they hold onto such a property, the more they lose, not only because of the costs, but also because it robs them the opportunity to invest in a better performing property. Therefore, in such situations, savvy investors admit they made a mistake, cut their losses, and direct whatever they salvaged from the poor investment into a better one. Similarly, when you realize you have made an investment that is costing you money, avoid the temptation to hold onto it. Cut your losses quickly before they balloon and scout for a better investment.

CHAPTER SEVEN: THE MOST IMPORTANT CHAPTER ON YOUR JOURNEY TOWARDS FINANCIAL FREEDOM

S o far, the previous chapters have provided you with all the information you need to start investing in real estate and embark on your journey toward financial independence. As I wind up, however, I want to share three steps that will increase your chances of success in the real estate sector and making enough money to achieve financial freedom.

Step 1: Build a Team

If you have enough money to finance your real estate investments, you can get started on your own. However, most of us are not born rich; therefore, most people do not have the funds to finance their investments on their own. Sure, you can always get a mortgage, but even then, you will need to pay a down payment on the property you want to invest in, and not everyone will have enough money saved up to cover that down payment. Even if you have the money, it could get where you require more funds than you can raise on your own. Aside from the financial aspect, it is unlikely you will have all the knowledge necessary to become successful in the real estate sector.

Therefore, my advice, as you prepare to get into real estate investing, is to start by building a team of professionals around you. If you talk to some of the wealthiest people on earth, most will tell you that, regardless of the business, they always surround themselves with a team of professionals. For instance, even if you get into the restaurant business, you cannot run your restaurant alone. You will need chefs, cooks, waiters, hosts, and so on. Even some of the richest people, like Bill Gates and Jeff Bezos, needed teams to help them build their empires. The same applies to me. I did not build my wealth on my own, but with the help of my team.

The greatest advantage of building a team is that it allows you to cut costs, which then leads to a healthier bottom line. You don't need huge amounts of money to start investing in real estate. For instance, if a property is selling at $150,000 and you have a team of 10 people, each of you would only need to raise $15,000, which is more attainable than raising $150,000 on your own.

When I was just getting started, I built a team of 20 people whom I trusted. We all put down $50,000, which instantly gave us access to $1 million to invest with. You don't have to have 20 people in your team necessarily, nor do you need to start with $50,000 each. You can start with something as low as $10,000 each, depending on the type of properties you intend to start with. You just need to raise enough money to cover the cost of purchasing the property, closing costs, and costs of renovating the property.

The beauty of coming together and raising enough money to purchase a property in cash is that you don't have to go through the headaches of qualifying for a mortgage loan. In addition, you get to save on all the interest that you would have paid on a loan.

When starting out, my team consisted of the following people:

- 1 Lawyer / Notary
- 4 Real-Estate Brokers
- 3 Mortgage Specialists (I was one of them)
- 3 General Contractors
- 1 Financial Advisor
- 1 Interior Decorator
- 1 Hotel Owner
- 1 Electrician
- 1 Plumber
- 1 Furniture Store Owner
- 1 Accountant
- 2 Students

As you can see, most of the people on my team were people who were closely linked to the real estate sector. This means that, aside from the money, they were also bringing in some professional expertise that would increase our chances of success. Likewise, when building your team, don't just focus on the money they can contribute—you should also think about the professional contribution they can make to the team. With my team, we were able to save on costs like real estate broker fees, renovations, décor, and so on because we had these professionals in the team. Of course, we also saved on interest because we did not use debt to finance our investment properties.

Although there is no limit to the number of people you can have on your team, it is advisable to aim for about 10-20 people. If the number becomes too small, you may be unable to raise enough money. Even if you did, you would probably only be able to invest in one property at a time. With 10-20 people, you can likely raise enough money to invest in 3-4 projects at a time. If the number becomes too high, the team could become too complicated to cooperate effectively.

Once you have formed your team, assign about 3 leaders to maintain control, and try to hold at least 2 meetings every month. This way, each member will be on the same page and up-to-date with what is going on. You can either hold the meetings on-site or through teleconferencing platforms like Skype, ZOOM, or TEAMS. You should approach this team like a group of professionals with a common agenda: making enough money to attain financial freedom, rather than just a group of friends. If you do this, it will be a lot easier for you to achieve success.

Step 2: Set Up a Company

Once you have put together your team, the next thing you need to do is to set up a company. There are several benefits that come with setting up a company. First, setting up a company formalizes the relationship between the members of the team. Second, it transfers liability from the individual team members to the company. Finally, a company could benefit from tax deductions that are other-wise unavailable to individual investors.

When it comes to setting up the company, it is advisable to either set up a Limited Liability Company (LLC) or Holding Company. An LLC is a corporation that protects the shareholders from liability for the company's debts. A Holding Company, on the other hand, is one that does not actively engage in business, such as the direct sale of goods or services (called an Operating Company). Instead, it simply holds equity interests or assets. Do not, under any circum-stances, buy investment properties with an Operating Company *(NEVER)*. If the operating company starts having problems and you go bankrupt, you will lose the properties registered under that company as well. Never put all your eggs in one basket.

When setting up your company, it is also good to seek the services of an accountant, lawyer, or notary to help with set up. In my case, my accountant did everything for me, and he ended up becoming one of my partners. Once you have picked a professional to help you set up the company, you will need to furnish them with all the partners' names and personal information, so they can register their names as shareholders. You will also need to decide which members will act as the company's President, Vice-President, Secretary, and Treasurer.

Once you are done setting up the company, the next thing you need to open the company's business account. For this, you will need to provide the company charter number to the bank. You will find the company charter number in the minute book provided to you by your accountant after the initial set up. It is always a good idea to set up the account such that 2 signatures will be required on all checks. Decide on the two partners who will be signing the checks on behalf of the company. In most cases, this will usually be the Treasurer and another official, such as the Secretary.

To confirm that all the team members are serious about becoming partners in the company, ask them to make a shareholder injection into the company (a check made out to the company's name). This initial deposit into the company can be taken out in the future and tax-free, since it was a shareholder's injection. Basically, what you put in, you can take out anytime without declaring it; it's your money, and taxes were already paid on that money prior to injecting it into the company. Speak to your accountant for more information—this is why it's important to have an accountant in your team.

The President of the company should be the Managing

Partner. In my case, I was the President because I was the one who built the team; *however*, never did I consider myself any higher or better than any one of my partners. We were all equal. I was the Managing Partner, and I had assigned four Senior Partners to help me out.

It is not an absolute necessity for you to hold the President position; it can be given to anyone who is capable. Actually, you can and *should* change roles every 2 years if one of the Partners decides that they would like to try that position. Of course, everything should be put to a vote. It is important that the Managing Partner keeps law and order in the everyday operations, so you should understand that the position is not made for everyone. It takes a team leader.

Once you are done setting up the company, creating a bank account, and choosing the company leadership team, it's time to move to the third step.

Step 3: Start Buying Properties

Now that you have your team ready, the company set up, and your business account open and hopefully full of cash, it's time to start scouting for investment properties that will make you money. This is where having some real estate brokers on your team comes in handy. If you have some brokers in your team, they will help you find the perfect property that will provide good returns and make your team money. The good thing is that there are deals everywhere— your team just needs to find them!

When it comes to making money from real estate, your team has 3 options:

• Buy low, renovate, and sell to make instant profits (flipping).

- Buy low, renovate, rent, and refinance (to pull out your initial investment to buy more properties while this property generates a revenue).

- Buy low, freshen up the property, and rent (to get a good return on your investment).

Any of these three simple options will work well for you and your team. You need to have a balance in your company, so that, at the end of the year, your company continues to generate revenue and expand your real estate portfolio. This is why I chose a team of 20 and started with $1 million. We allocated enough funds to all three techniques of making money in real estate. Before we got to the second and third method, I made sure that we did 2-3 flips, so we had enough cash to keep some of our properties and not be forced to sell them. You can also use this approach, or you can find another that works better for you.

The most important thing I want you to keep in mind as I close this chapter is that, if you want to start with the little you have and build a real estate empire, you need a strong team. It doesn't matter how rich or poor the team members are, as long as they can contribute to the success of the company's goal of financial freedom through real estate. A group of 18-year-olds can start this with almost no money and create an empire. It's so simple that your kids can do it simply by applying everything that you learned from this book.

IF YOU ENJOYED THIS BOOK AND YOU LEARNED SOMETHING NEW, PLEASE DON'T FORGET TO LEAVE ME A POSITIVE REVIEW ONLINE, IT

WOULD MEAN THE WORLD TO ME. THANK YOU
VERY MUCH! :-)

Visit my website at <u>www.TheBestSellerBooks.com</u> to see
my other books available and to follow me on Social
Media

FINAL WORDS

When you began reading this book, I promised you that I would give you knowledge that would help you stop being overly reliant on your job—where you are highly expendable and where you can never be too sure whether you'll be able to sustain yourself if the cost of living keeps rising—and take full control of your life. Throughout the course of this book, I provided you with knowledge, strategies, and techniques that will help you do precisely that, and by investing in real estate and attaining financial freedom.

In Chapter 1, I explained financial freedom and shared the foundational steps that will help kickstart your journey to financial independence. These steps include spending less than you earn, cutting down your expenses, paying off your debt, finding ways to increase your income, making the right investments with your money, and, finally, computing how much money you need to sustain yourself and figuring out how your investments can generate this money.

In Chapter 2, I covered the basics of real estate investing, including how people make money in real estate, the factors that affect the real estate market, risks associated with real estate investing, different types of real estate you can invest in, and various ways through which you can invest in real estate.

In Chapter 3, I went over the various aspects of finding a suitable property to invest in, including where to find rental properties for sale, the criteria for selecting suitable properties to invest in, importance of doing your due diligence before deciding to invest in a property, how to decide if the price of a property is acceptable, and how to crunch the numbers and determine if the property will be profitable.

In Chapter 4, I shared the different options you have for financing your investment property, such as using your own cash, getting a conventional mortgage, getting FHA loans, applying for asset-based loans, leveraging your home equity, second home financing, lease options, and mortgage assumption.

In Chapter 5, I covered the basics of renting out and managing your rental property. We went over things like how to prepare your home for renters, find tenants for your property, choose the right tenants, create a good lease agreement, advantages of working with a property manager and their roles, importance of keeping your property well-maintained, common problems you will likely encounter when managing a rental property, and how to handle your tax obligations.

In Chapter 6, I went over various tactics to help you expand your portfolio and inch closer to financial freedom. We looked at how to determine the number of properties you need in your portfolio, the different tactics for quickly growing your portfolio, the importance of diversifying your portfolio, how to increase the value of your properties, and the importance of having an investment strategy.

Finally, in Chapter 7, I provided you with three simple steps that will help you transform your desire for financial independence through real estate investing from a dream into reality.

Now that you have come to the end of this book, you have all the information you need to take control of your life, break free from the chains of employment, and attain financial independence. All that is remaining for you now is to go out and put into practice everything you have learned from this book. The good thing is that the information in this book has been explained simply enough that even a kid can understand and implement it. Financial independence is within your reach, and, as long as you make the commitment to put into practice what I have taught you, I can promise you that you will get there. Anyone can do it, and certainly, *you* can do it!

Lastly, if you loved the content in this book, and if it has been helpful to you, I would really appreciate it if you left a positive review.

All the best as you get started on your journey to *__financial freedom with real estate!__*

∿

IF YOU ENJOYED THIS BOOK AND YOU LEARNED SOMETHING NEW, PLEASE DON'T FORGET TO LEAVE ME A POSITIVE REVIEW ONLINE, IT WOULD MEAN THE WORLD TO ME. THANK YOU VERY MUCH! :-)

Visit __www.TheBestSellerBooks.com__ to see my other books and to follow me.

∿

FINANCIAL FREEDOM CHECKLIST

(A Simple list that should be followed to the "T")

This checklist includes:

❏ 9 important steps that you should follow to achieve success and head toward *Financial Freedom With Real Estate*

❏ Plus receive future updates

Forget about yesterday and start thinking about tomorrow!

> *"The past and the future are separated by a second,*
> *so make that second count!"*
> —Carmine Pirone

To receive your Financial Freedom With Real Estate checklist, email me at:

michael@TheBestSellerBooks.com

REFERENCES

A. (2019, August 27). Criteria for Choosing an Investment Property. Retrieved May 31, 2020, from https://www.makescents.com.au/criteria-for-choosing-an-investment-property/

Adams, R. L. (2019a, May 24). 8 Proven Ways to Make Money in Real Estate. Retrieved May 29, 2020, from https://www.entrepreneur.com/article/298748

Adams, R. L. (2019b, May 24). 8 Proven Ways to Make Money in Real Estate. Retrieved June 1, 2020, from https://www.entrepreneur.com/article/298748

Anneken Tappe, CNN Business. (2020, April 30). 30 million Americans have filed initial unemployment claims since mid-March. Retrieved May 29, 2020, from https://edition.cnn.com/2020/04/30/economy/unemployment-benefits-coronavirus/index.html

Average Sales Price for New Houses Sold in the United States. (2020, May 26). Retrieved May 29, 2020, from https://fred.stlouisfed.org/series/ASPNHSUS

Bay Property Management Group. (2020, March 2). 6 Common Problems Landlords Face and How to Fix Them.

Retrieved June 4, 2020, from https://www.baymgmtgroup.-com/blog/6-common-problems-landlords-face-and-how-to-fix-them/

Boykin, R. (2020, April 15). Reasons to Invest in Real Estate vs. Stocks. Retrieved May 28, 2020, from https://www.in-vestopedia.com/investing/reasons-invest-real-estate-vs-stock-market/

Brumer-Smith, L. (2020a, May 12). Rental Properties. Retrieved May 30, 2020, from https://www.fool.com/mil-lionacres/real-estate-investing/rental-properties/

Brumer-Smith, L. (2020b, May 12). Rental Property Investing Basics. Retrieved June 3, 2020, from https://www.-fool.com/millionacres/real-estate-investing/rental-properties/

Carson, C. (2019a, August 20). The Rental Debt Snowball Plan - How to Get Free & Clear Rental Properties. Retrieved June 2, 2020, from https://www.coachcarson.com/debt-snowball-plan/

Carson, C. (2019b, November 8). Dave Ramsey Says Debt is Dumb in Real Estate Investing. Is It True? Retrieved June 2, 2020, from https://www.coachcarson.com/dave-ramsey-debt-is-dumb-real-estate/

Davis, B. G. (2019, May 20). Survey of Millionaires Reveals 7 Habits: How Many Do You Have? | SparkRental. Retrieved May 29, 2020, from https://sparkrental.com/survey-habits-millionaires/

DiLallo, M. (2020, June 1). Real Estate 101: What Is Peer-to-Peer Lending? Retrieved June 2, 2020, from https://www.-fool.com/millionacres/real-estate-financing/real-estate-101-what-peer-peer-lending/

Elkins, K. (2017, February 6). The way Arnold Schwarzenegger made his first million had nothing to do with acting. Retrieved May 29, 2020, from https://www.cn-bc.com/2017/02/06/the-way-arnold-schwarzenegger-made-his-first-million.html

Frankel, M. C. (2019, June 9). Buying Your First Investment Property: A Step-by-Step Guide. Retrieved June 1, 2020, from https://www.fool.com/millionacres/real-estate-investing/rental-properties/buying-your-first-investment-property-step-step-guide/

Frankel, M. C. (2020, June 9). Buying Your First Investment Property: A Step-by-Step Guide. Retrieved May 31, 2020, from https://www.fool.com/millionacres/real-estate-investing/rental-properties/buying-your-first-investment-property-step-step-guide/

FRED Economic Data. (2020, May 26). Retrieved May 29, 2020, from https://fred.stlouisfed.org/series/USSTHPI

Garcia, A. (2019, June 2). A Proven Formula For Buying Rental Properties. Retrieved May 30, 2020, from https://www.moneyunder30.com/formula-buying-rental-properties

Golhar, A. (2017, November 9). Why Real Estate Investors Should Consider Lease Options. Retrieved June 3, 2020, from https://www.forbes.com/sites/forbesrealestatecouncil/2017/11/09/why-real-estate-investors-should-consider-lease-options/#448ee1bf1a78

Greene, D. (2018a, November 27). Why Real Estate Builds Wealth More Consistently Than Other Asset Classes. Retrieved May 30, 2020, from https://www.forbes.com/sites/davidgreene/2018/11/27/why-real-estate-builds-wealth-more-consistently-than-other-asset-classes/#2fe720265405

Greene, D. (2018b, December 27). House Hacking: How Financially Savvy People Live in Expensive Markets While Saving Money. Retrieved June 2, 2020, from https://www.forbes.com/sites/davidgreene/2018/12/04/house-hacking-how-financially-savvy-people-live-in-expensive-markets-while-saving-money/#53f8952c70f0

Hamed, E. (2019, November 10). Is Buying Foreclosed

Homes a Smart Real Estate Investment? Retrieved May 31, 2020, from https://www.mashvisor.com/blog/buying-foreclosed-homes-smart-investment/

Harris, J. (2017, November 16). 5 Reasons Why Real Estate Is a Great Investment. Retrieved May 28, 2020, from https://www.entrepreneur.com/article/304860

Hoffower, H. (2020, September 11). Meet the typical millennial millionaire in America, who has a real-estate portfolio worth $1.4 million, is married, and is more likely to live in California than any other state. Retrieved May 29, 2020, from https://www.businessinsider.com/typical-american-millennial-millionaire-net-worth-building-wealth-2019-11

Josephson, A. (2018, June 25). FHA vs. Conventional Loans. Retrieved June 1, 2020, from https://smartasset.com/mortgage/fha-vs-conventional-loans

Julia Horowitz, CNN Business. (2020, May 3). Stocks week ahead: May 3, 2020. Retrieved May 29, 2020, from https://edition.cnn.com/2020/05/03/investing/stocks-week-ahead/index.html

Karani, A. (2019, October 24). How to Grow Your Real Estate Investment Portfolio in 2020. Retrieved June 4, 2020, from https://www.mashvisor.com/blog/grow-real-estate-investment-portfolio-2020/

Kennon, J. (2020, March 9). Real Estate Investing for Beginners. Retrieved May 29, 2020, from https://www.thebalance.com/real-estate-investing-101-357985

Khoury, M. (2018a, April 25). 4 Things to Know Before Investing in Real Estate. Retrieved May 30, 2020, from https://www.mashvisor.com/blog/4-things-know-before-investing-in-real-estate/

Khoury, M. (2018b, April 25). 4 Things to Know Before Investing in Real Estate. Retrieved June 3, 2020, from https://www.mashvisor.com/blog/4-things-know-before-investing-in-real-estate/

Kielar, H. (2019, August 5). What Is Mortgage Assumption And Why Might You Do It? Retrieved June 1, 2020, from https://www.quickenloans.com/learn/what-is-mortgage-assumption-and-why-might-you-do-it

LaMagna, M. (2019, August 16). Forget retirement — focus on financial independence. Retrieved May 28, 2020, from https://www.marketwatch.com/story/forget-golf-and-grand-kids-retirement-is-really-about-financial-independence-at-any-age-2019-05-23

Leonhardt, M. (2019, May 13). 62% of millennials say they're living paycheck to paycheck. Retrieved May 27, 2020, from https://www.cnbc.com/2019/05/10/62-percent-of-millennials-say-they-are-living-paycheck-to-paycheck.html

McCarthy, B. J. (2019, June 12). Stock Investments Lose Some Luster After COVID-19 Sell-Off. Retrieved May 28, 2020, from https://news.gallup.com/poll/309233/stock-investments-lose-luster-covid-sell-off.aspx

McLean, R. (2014, March 14). How To Buy More Property – 10 Ways To Boost Your Portfolio. Retrieved June 4, 2020, from https://onproperty.com.au/how-to-buy-more-property/

Merrill, T. (2019, January 15). Achieving Financial Independence With Real Estate. Retrieved May 27, 2020, from https://www.thanmerrill.com/financial-independence/

Oracles, T. C. (2019, October 2). Real estate is still the best investment you can make today, millionaires say—here's why. Retrieved May 28, 2020, from https://www.cnbc.com/2019/10/01/real-estate-is-still-the-best-investment-you-can-make-today-millionaires-say.html

O'Shea, A. (2020, May 22). How to Invest in Real Estate: 5 Ways to Get Started. Retrieved May 29, 2020, from https://www.nerdwallet.com/blog/investing/5-ways-to-invest-in-real-estate/

Palmer, B. (2020, April 14). Key Reasons to Invest in Real Estate. Retrieved May 28, 2020, from https://www.investopedia.com/articles/mortgages-real-estate/11/key-reasons-invest-real-estate.asp

Paquin, P. (2017, February 19). Retirement Statistics That Might Change How You View Retirement. Retrieved May 28, 2020, from https://reachfinancialindependence.com/retirement-statistics-might-change-view-retirement/

Petrov, C. (2019, June 10). 12 Personal Finance Statistics to Set Your Goals in 2020. Retrieved May 29, 2020, from https://spendmenot.com/personal-finance-statistics/

Pitarre, A. (2020, March 9). A Look at Wealth 2019: Millennial Millionaires. Retrieved May 29, 2020, from https://blog.coldwellbankerluxury.com/a-look-at-wealth-millennial-millionaires/

Property Lease Options Explained –. (2020, February 20). Retrieved June 1, 2020, from https://www.propertygeek.net/article/property-lease-options-explained/

Rose, J. (2018, October 15). The 15 Crucial Steps Needed To Achieve Financial Independence. Retrieved May 28, 2020, from https://www.forbes.-com/sites/jrose/2016/03/25/financial-independence/#2ae5c25984b3

Rumora, B. E. (2019, June 7). 5 Tips for Owning Low-Income Rentals. Retrieved June 4, 2020, from https://www.biggerpockets.com/blog/build-real-estate-portfolio-fast-the-stack

Rumora, B. E. (2020, February 7). 5 Tips for Owning Low-Income Rentals. Retrieved June 3, 2020, from https://www.biggerpockets.com/blog/hire-property-manager

Stephan, G. (2019, May 1). How to Retire Early from Real Estate Investing. Retrieved May 28, 2020, from https://www.youtube.com/watch?v=t-5veYUeatw

Supino, K. (2020, April 14). How to Leverage the 1031 Exchange to Grow Your Wealth. Retrieved June 4, 2020, from https://www.mashvisor.com/blog/leverage-1031-exchange-grow-wealth/

Turner, B. B. (2019, June 8). Quit Your Day Job and Find Financial Freedom: Here's How to Become a Real Estate Investor (Full-Time!). Retrieved June 2, 2020, from https://www.biggerpockets.com/blog/real-estate-investing-partnerships-powerful

Yates, J. (2020, February 11). 90% of the World's Millionaires Do This to Create Wealth. Retrieved May 29, 2020, from https://thecollegeinvestor.com/11300/90-percent-worlds-millionaires-do-this/

Printed in Great Britain
by Amazon